ONE CHILLY SIBERIAN MORNING

DOUGLAS BOTTING

ONE CHILLY SIBERIAN MORNING

Photographs by John Bayliss and Douglas Botting
Drawings by Leslie W. Botting

THE MACMILLAN COMPANY · NEW YORK

Library of Congress Catalog Card Number: 67-14415

First American Edition

THE MACMILLAN COMPANY, NEW YORK
COLLIER-MACMILLAN CANADA LTD.,
TORONTO, ONTARIO

Printed in the United States of America

TO
LOUISE MY WIFE

CONTENTS

ILLUSTRATIONS

I

In Vadim's Town

ONE chilly Siberian morning, snug in my sleeping-bag of furs, I woke to the cries of the migrating birds and the soft swish of their wings as they passed overhead. It was June, but still the grey clouds rolled in low from the sea and the snow swirled across the sunless spaces and danced in the window. I got up and put on my felt *velenkies* and my hat of reindeer calf, fortified myself with the scraps of last night's reindeer stew, picked up my gun, slung a bandolier of shells over my shoulder, ducked through the tent flap and strode out across the snowy marshes as if I had done so every day of my life. I was aware of no incongruity that morning. The grey wigwams of the lonely encampment behind me, the wind-burned herdsman passing by on his sledge, the reindeer herd grazing on the distant skyline, the waste land stretching ahead—all seemed the natural and inevitable components of my life then, and I did not question them. I did not question the fact that I should be hunting wildfowl in such a remote and improbable region of the Soviet Union, 4,000 miles from Moscow and on exactly the other side of the world from home, nor did I question anything else about that unlikely morning—the scurrying flight of the northern birds across the lake, the crack of guns in the silence, the skin-clad Siberian retrieving fallen duck fom a kayak, the splintered sun peering icily down on a world of moss and snow and water. Only later did the absurdity come home to me; only then did I begin to wonder. How had all this come to pass?

It began, as I recall, the morning Vadim came when we were having breakfast in our room overlooking Moscow's Sverdlov Square.

It was a strange room. Pillars of marble rose like polished stalagmites to a ceiling of yellowing ornamental plaster. A huge chandelier hung low over the table and tinkled gently in the draught from the window. From the sombre walls hung an enormous, gilt-framed mirror and paintings whose oils had long since faded into an antique gloom. Nothing seemed to have changed since the previous century. Every stick of furniture, every item of bric-à-brac—the Ming vase, the thickly tasselled lampshades, the great settle, the rich and tattered window drapes, the escritoire with its impedimenta of heavy green marble—all cried out from the past, demanding recognition after such prolonged neglect, waiting for me to doff my plebeian cap. When I heard the knock on the door and the rattle of the doorknob, I had almost expected some hiccupping nobleman to come teetering giddily in, or to hear a rustle of silk as some adulterous grand duchess returned to the room she had only recently vacated. But when I looked up from my breakfast it was no ghost I saw advancing towards me.

Vadim, nevertheless, was a shock. As he strode into the room, one hand cheerily extended as if we were long-lost buddies, he greeted us in a broad East-Coast American accent, faultless in its nasality and long-drawn vowels. "Hi, you guys!" he hailed us cheerily. "Welcome to Moscow." We blinked at him disbelievingly over our toast. "What's going on, you fellers? Everything dandy? Rooms are swell, aren't they? Folks call me Vadim—Novosty Agency."

Novosty was the Russian Press Agency that had, in a sense, sponsored our visit to the Soviet Union, or at any rate made itself responsible for arrangements during our stay; it was a newly-formed organisation to which all itinerant foreign correspondents and photographers were directed on their arrival in Moscow. What I had not expected was that our Novosty man should be such a perfect take-off of an American news-hawk.

The crew-cut, the heavy horn-rimmed spectacles, the buttoned-down collar, the neatly cut grey suit, and both the aspect and mannerisms of one who had just dropped in from Manhattan were a surprise.

"I'm John Bayliss," my companion said, half-risen from his chair and wiping the egg from his mouth.

"Pleased to meet you, John."

"And I'm Douglas Botting," I said.

"Hi, Doug. Now listen, fellers, I haven't got much time. I've got to go to Leningrad to take a few pictures. I thought I'd just drop by and see you were fixed up OK."

"Everything couldn't be better," John said.

"Oh, that's fine. Say, are those cigarettes Stuyvesant? Let's have a pack, will you, fellers? Now listen, I've got an idea . . ."

We came to know Vadim well in the months that followed. He had been born in France, the son of an official in the Soviet Embassy in Paris. At the age of eighteen he had started to learn English at the Foreign Languages Institute in Moscow. Graduated from there, he was sent to the United States as an interpreter at a world fair, and later he came to London as Press Officer for the Leningrad Symphony Orchestra. Now he was cast in the role of photographer and wore hanging from his shoulder like a badge of office a Japanese Pentax, acquired somehow from some Western pressman, which was held together by pieces of sticking-plaster.

In his private life Vadim toyed with athletics ("I am second-rate," he once told us, which seemed to be an official category rather than a self-deprecatory opinion), and lived with his wife ("She pecks me") and small son in a flat he shared with two other families. He was one of the few Russians I ever met who owned a car—at least he said he owned it—a limping blue thing with a radio, a luxury item he was never tired of demonstrating. "You see, guys," he would say as he filled the car with electronic whistles through which one could just detect the familiar warm throbbing of Louis Armstrong's trumpet, "I can get the Voice of America on this set. Can you hear it? *Jazz Hour, USA*—a great programme." He was, in his way, a boyish Americophile and yet, I reflected, he could hardly keep his job, with its unusual opportunities for foreign travel and foreign contacts, without being a very reliable Communist as well. This was a subject we could never broach with him. "Oh hell, fellers," he would exclaim if the conversation teetered dangerously near it, "don't let's talk politics, it's too boring." Beneath the cheery bonhomie there was, I felt, an intelligence sticking with Jesuitical conviction to orthodox beliefs. But we liked him a lot, and he was always full of bright ideas.

"Listen, I've got an idea," he said as he sat at our table that first morning. "Your interest is out-of-the-way places and an adventurous life, right? Well, how would you like it if we sent you to Siberia?"

"You mean . . . ?"

"Yeah. Beyond the Ural Mountains. Across the big divide. Into the great new outback. Boy, that's some country! How would you like to go?"

We had arrived in Moscow with no clear idea of our itinerary through the Soviet Union. Such things had been impossible to arrange in London and it was only in Moscow that we might learn what could or could not be permitted to foreign travellers in the Soviet Union. Now, it seemed, Vadim was the man delegated to give us our marching orders.

"I've always wanted to see a salt mine," John said, a smile creeping with difficulty across his face.

"Leave it to me, fellers. I'll fix it," Vadim said. And shortly he was gone.

Thus it was, round a table littered with egg-shells and black bread, that the seeds of our journey were sown. Outside the traffic in Sverdlov Square purred gently, and loudspeakers, like owls in the leafless plane trees, hooted the strident martial music of May Day. Eastwards stretched the limitless forests and steppes of the largest nation on earth. We were anxious to go.

It is nearly midnight by the Kremlin clock and the headlamps of tanks and rocket-carriers illuminate Red Square and St. Basil's Cathedral during a rehearsal for the May Day parade.

The clandestine photograph of the courtroom at the beginning of the Wynne–Penkowski spy trial in Moscow. The three judges are in the centre, the accused at the far right.

We had come to Russia to make a film. I had known John Bayliss ever since we had been at Oxford together and he was an expert and fluent Russian speaker. For my part, I had spent a large proportion of my time since those days travelling to the remoter corners of the world, writing and photographing, and it was in the capacity of special correspondents for the BBC that we had set out for Moscow that early springtime.

John had been to the Soviet Union before and had therefore known what to expect. It was he who had first broached the idea of an expedition there to me and had made the arrangements to put it into effect. At first I had viewed it with some apprehension. Russia for me was a conglomeration of preconceptions and prejudices, of images remembered from childhood reading, wartime newsreels and items gleaned in maturity from the Western press. Russia was wolves and bears and troikas in silent, gleaming wastes of snow; Nihilists plotting, Napoleon retreating, princes dancing in the glittering ballrooms of St Petersburg palaces. Russia was piles of frozen corpses on the Finnish frontier, tanks scything through Ukrainian wheatlands, soldiers running through blazing streets, Stalingrad. Russia was the knock on the door at midnight, a volley of shots in the courtyard, the hopelessness of the forced labour camps, Stalin. It was the Berlin airlift, Budapest, *nyet* in the Security Council, fear of war. It was monstrous, hairy women throwing javelins; melancholy choirs; brilliant humourless dancers; novelists writing party handouts; Pasternak. Russia was record production figures, seven-year plans, hero workers, Orders of Lenin; it was *pogrom, sputnik, tovarich*, and *borshch*. Russia was a name that triggered off a chain reaction of images; a variety of vague emotions and an odd assortment of patchy, imprecise facts coloured my attitudes.

At the same time, while the image I had formed of the USSR was a frightening one, it seemed to me foolish not to avail myself of an opportunity to travel widely in that country and to see at first-hand what there might be behind the claims and counter-claims, the accusations and denials and all the extravagant rubbish with which we are daily bombarded by the propaganda machines of East and West. I wanted to see what Communism was about, for at times it seemed to offer some sort of way out of the mess of the old order, to provide (as war sometimes provides) a moral climate where there were other causes to nail one's colours to than self-interest and pecuniary gain. And I wanted to meet Russians; I did not believe that they could possibly resemble the cropped-headed, bull-necked, bully-jawed thugs of Western newspaper cartoons any more than they resembled the absurdly grinning, contented, tall, strong, blond, pure-in-mind-and-body heroes of the Soviet hand-outs. I had only met one Red Russian in my life, a Cultural Attaché at the Soviet Embassy in London, who had the unusual privilege of being allowed to mix socially with English people. He was urbane, smartly dressed and rather humourless; he played chess simultaneously on two boards and would win both games every time. He did nothing to belie my preconceptions of the Russian people, to pin an individual face to the Soviet cardboard cut-out, and when the Christine Keeler scandal started he was recalled to Moscow.

.   .   .

John and I had reached Russia in late April, and we settled down in the grand old Hotel Metropole in Moscow to endure the interminable wait for our visas to Siberia. During that period occurred an event which has etched its memory into my brain like acid.

On May 5th we had received press passes to attend the trial of an Englishman, Greville Wynne, and a Russian, Oleg Penkowski, on charges of espionage against the Soviet Union. At 9.30 on May 7th we arrived at the court for the first day of the proceedings.

It was clearly stated on the back of our passes that no photography was permitted, but Vadim, for reasons best known to himself, suggested that we disregard these orders, and told us how to smuggle our cameras into the courtroom. We sat at the back of the room until two minutes before the trial was due to start at ten a.m. and then walked to the front of the court, immediately

to the right of the judges' bench, where the Soviet film and TV
cameras were. The place was like a film set, with big banks of
lights and spotlights directed on the positions of the individual
performers and the various benches arranged theatrically to suit the
cameras.

Wynne and Penkowski came in after the judges. It was a horrid
feeling, watching one's fellow countryman in a Soviet court, and I
felt almost traitorous turning my camera on him. Wynne blinked
in the bright lights and squinted at the crowd in a strange,
unnerving way. But he quickly recovered his composure and began
to answer the questions crisply and firmly. Where was he born,
where did he live, what was his job, his qualifications? I felt
miserable for him: he should have been in a pub, drinking a pint
and talking of cricket, not mixed up in this charade. My hands
were trembling—I was standing in full view of the court with a
camera I had no right to bring there: if I reached out I could touch
the sleeve of one of the judges. John, I saw, was transfixed behind a
gigantic camera with a lens like a gun. I moved my position to the
front row of seats, next to Penkowski. He was very dignified and
calm—yet he would be shot: "Are you coming back on Saturday
for the death sentence?" Vadim asked me later.

We left the court at eleven. Immediately outside the courtroom
door was a buffet with fruit and cake on sale. It was, I learned, the
only place where you could buy pineapples in Moscow.

I mention this event because, though strictly it had little to do
with the journey which is the subject of the book, it made a
strong impact on both of us. It made us very anxious to depart at
once for the Siberian wilderness and leave the claustrophobic
atmosphere of Moscow; and it reminded us that, however far we
were to travel in this vast land, it would always remain an alien
country. To go east was to go further from home than the sum of
the miles we would travel.

2

Wake me up at Omsk

I SAT alone in our room in the Hotel Metropole, waiting for
John to come back with the air-tickets to Irkutsk. We had aimed
to catch the 3.15 afternoon flight but Vadim, expected at noon,
didn't arrive till gone two. Oblivious of our urgency and pressing
schedule, he said he was hungry, he hadn't eaten all day and he
would like to sink his teeth into some meat. John ordered soup,
pies, three helpings of boeuf Stroganoff and some beer, and as we
sat round the table scoffing our meal and looking at our watches
in a pointed manner, Vadim relaxed and treated us to a lecture on
what to expect and what to do and what not to do in Siberia.

"Whatever you do," Vadim said, "don't go around photographing little old ladies. Or little old men. They won't like it
and, besides, they're not typical, if you see what I mean. And I've
no need to tell you fellows not to take pictures at railway stations,
or airports, or bridges or military installations or any of those
kind of things. It's not that there's anything special, probably,
but it's against the law. If you're ever in any doubt, ask permission,
or don't shoot. And don't go around—do you think we could
order some more beer?—don't go around asking a lot of questions,
because maybe some of those guys out there haven't seen too
many foreigners and they've got their heads full of spy stories.
You know what I mean. I mean they're not so—uh—sophisticated
as the fellows you meet in Moscow, they think there are spies all
over the place and every foreigner may be a spy, and don't go
around—Leningradskoye beer, John, it's stronger. What time did
you say your plane was? I'm sorry, fellers, you're not ever going to
make it. What about the next one? What I was going to say was,

don't go around in fancy costume as if you'd just come out of Savile Row (is that it?), I mean wearing awfully smart clothes and suits and so on, because they're not used to that sort of thing in Siberia and you'll only attract attention to yourself. You don't want to attract attention to yourself. Now . . . ''

Vadim had his feet up on the table. There was meat in his stomach and a full glass of beer in his hand. He seemed very content and he was still talking when it was time for our plane to take off. We sat there saying, "Yes, Vadim," and "No, of course not, Vadim," and Vadim started to reminisce about the time *he* was in Siberia. It was a lovely country, he said.

"Take Lake Baikal, now, that's beautiful, that's really a great place. You can take some beautiful pictures of the scenery around there. Further north, though, it gets rougher. If I were you I'd take some cans of food—canned meat and fish and vegetables, you can get them in the *Gastronom*—because in Yakutsk, I remember, there's really only one restaurant so it's always full, and you get in to town late in the evening and you're cold and tired and you don't want to wait for hours—you *can* do there, wait for hours till you get served—but if you have your own cans you can have *something* to eat straight off. That's what I'd do, next time. Oh, it's rough out there all right. Oh yes. And another thing—I must be going—keep your Stuyvesant cigarettes. They'll come in very handy as bribes. You've sent off the cable for a hotel reservation in Irkutsk? You've got your plane tickets? No? Then you couldn't have caught the three o'clock plane anyway, could you?"

When he had gone we sat for a while despondently amongst our packed cases and locked and labelled boxes while through the double-glazed windows filtered the drone of the afternoon traffic in Sverdlov Square, the pulse of the city from which I so much wanted to escape. Escape *to* Siberia. It seemed bizarre.

The maid came in after a while to clear away the debris of our lunch. "Are you still here?" she scolded. "Not yet gone to the Virgin Lands and the North Pole and all those exciting places? Then stay and get drunk with us." It was an idea, it was how we felt, but while there was still a chance of catching the late afternoon flight to Irkutsk we could not let up. John set off for the Aeroflot office and I stayed behind and made a phone-call to London.

A phone-call, even one between Moscow and London that has to be re-diverted through Prague, does not take up all one's time, and after I had made it it was evident that John was taking a very long time to buy a couple of air-tickets and there was nothing for me to do but sit and wait. I tried to read a novel by Graham Greene, a story of passion on the wrong side of Clapham Common, but it seemed too remote from my present mood and I got up and stared through the window at the streets that were blackening now in the drizzle that fell from a chill, grey, springtime Moscow sky. Escape *to* Siberia? Yes, I thought, yes. Even to there.

What was this place we were going to, this huge, empty hunk of the map that was still only a name, an idea, a hive of buzzing preconceptions? Siberia. Alone in that strange hotel room, with nothing better to do, I turned the name over in my mind, sampled it like a lozenge on my tongue, tried to evoke some kind of a picture that could replace the worrying blank of unknowingness, the vacuum in my brain. It was certainly an evocative place-name. I could hear the wind in it, the hiss of the snow across the ice, the sigh in the cedars, the swish of the sledge-runners across the frozen river, the searing blizzard screaming over open spaces. It was an apt name, very onomatopoeic; like a stone tossed into a pool, it set up a ring of ripples, circles of connotations. Siberia. Frozen and bleeding feet wrapped in paper and sacking drag their terrible way over the endless steppes; hands clutch the barbed wire of the slave-camp perimeter, ward off the descending rifle-butt and the rawhide whip. In my mind's eye were the grey, blank faces of the unjustly sentenced and the eternally hopeless; the guard's bark, the rifle echoing in the wilderness, the cut-throat glare of the searchlight in the sentry tower, the silence like death. Or again, the salmon leaping into the brown bear's paw and the ragged wolves skulking in the brushwood, howling at an icy, cut-glass moon; and the hunter, a beard and two eyes within a hoop of furs, setting traps for sable; and the miners of salt and of gold, with hands like gorillas', roaring for vodka, for women, for blood . . .

But was Siberia at all like this? How closely could it resemble my fancy? To judge from what little Vadim had told us, it was a land peopled by little old men and little old women, aged dwarfs who inhabited bridges and railway stations and objected to snapshots; a raw land where the restaurants never served food and anyone would do anything for a drag of a Stuyvesant cigarette. Or had I got it all wrong? Reluctantly I decided I knew nothing of Siberia, that John and I, with monumental unpreparedness, were about to plunge into a void which was, as I could see from my map, somewhat larger than the entire United States of America. The prospect was daunting.

It was early evening by the time John returned; he had been away three hours, and came back bad-tempered and empty-handed. It was the usual story of bureaucratic confusion and ineptitude; though he had paid for the tickets, he had never actually been given them; he had been passed from one office to another, from Intourist to Aeroflot and back again, and each time he had received the same indifferent response, the same evasive statement or hollow promise; there was no problem in obtaining passages to Siberia, for we had our visas and Press Department permits, it was just that one official alone, even one office alone, was insufficiently empowered by itself to book the seats and the flight, issue the tickets and receive payment for them; and when it came to the crunch, when our aeroplane had long since flown away and the offices were closing at the end of the day's work, John was informed that, unfortunately, he couldn't have his ticket because it was "somewhere between here and the airport". He was livid, for he had had to bear the brunt of this tiresome performance. I was just depressed. How could they ever hope for a big tourist industry in this country, I asked, when to get something as elementary as an air-ticket was like applying for an income tax rebate? But my real anger was at having to spend another night in Moscow. That was unpardonable, unbearable.

Two days later we drove out to the airport, the one for domestic
flights at Sheremetevo. It was the end of May and a day redolent
of summer promise. The sun shone brightly from a clear sky and
the air was warm. In the streets of the suburbs I could see that at
last the women had discarded their heavy skirts and woollies and
drab coats and were venturing out in summer frocks that had
lain in drawers for the past six months, while the men were now
walking around in shirt-sleeves and straw hats. The countryside
beyond the suburbs had changed remarkably since I had last seen
it only a week or so previously, for it was green now, with the
bright, fresh greenness of emergent leaves and newly-sprouted
grass; the gardens of the empty wooden houses along the road—
houses due for demolition in the path of the advancing blocks of
pre-fabricated flats—seemed suddenly to have exploded with a
jungly profusion of rank weeds and tall flowers gone to seed; and
the new leaves of the forest flickered in the breeze like a million
semaphores. Down by the river-bank, which not so long ago had
harboured the last defiant, doomed vestiges of the winter ice,
families were picnicking beside their parked cars, and ample
Russian bodies in bathing costumes walked along the roadside
clutching butterfly nets; in the undergrowth among the silver
birches near the road lovers lay together, one face against another
under the trees, seasonal passions caught briefly in a snapshot
glimpse from our rattling taxi. There was, too, an unfamiliar
odour coming from the forest around the airport, a summer smell
of earth and leaves and pine gum, of swamp drying out and dust
blowing, a new exciting aroma pervading an archetypal Russian
landscape.

The passenger building at Sheremetevo Domestic was a
seething, bawling microcosm of the Soviet Empire. Here, momentarily assembled, were representatives of all the far-flung regions
of this sprawling nation—Uzbeks and Georgians, Tadjiks and
Estonians, men of Turkmenistan, of the Mongolian frontier,
of the mountains of Kirghiziya. This motley crowd—a bedlam of
tongues and chaos of slit-eyes and oriental beards—jostled in
doorways and at check-in counters or lay sprawled along wooden

benches amongst a litter of battered suit-cases and lumpy cloth
bundles in an agony of patience. From time to time an announcement over the public address system would stifle a score of yawns,
and a kind of collective shiver would go through the comatose
company of waiting passengers; they would rouse themselves and
stumble, bumping and boring each other in a frenzy of felt boots
and Asiatic slippers, towards the departure bays. It was a very
strange, restless, noisy place, this clearing-house of empire; if
ancient Rome had had an airport it could not have contained a
more variegated crowd of citizens than this; and it was strange to
think that, though this airport was solely for the purpose of
domestic flights within the Soviet Union, some of the flights
would be as long as ones between London and Johannesburg,
Chicago, Calcutta or Panama.

Our plane to Irkutsk was due to leave at 3.30, but our first
attempt to board it was abortive. The flight departure had been
duly announced and we had clambered into a curious "train" of
little trolley-cars with our extraordinary mound of hand-baggage.
But instead of going to the aircraft we were driven on an absurd
tour of the airfield, past TU-104s and Ilyushin-18s and beneath
the wing of the monstrous TU-114 (eight propellers and 220
passengers), before returning to our starting place. "What's the
matter?" a fellow-traveller, an engineer bound for Bratsk, asked
one of the Aeroflot girls. "Nothing," she replied. "It is just that
the plane is not ready." And our companion turned to us with a
shrug and said, sadly, "What can you do? Where Aeroflot begins,
order ends."

It was an hour later before we finally did take off and rose with
a scream of jet engines into the hazy sky of a hot afternoon.
Forests and towns receded beneath us; soon we were at 24,000
feet, viewing the earth like little gods in a tin box roaring through
space. "Wake me up at Omsk," the Bratsk engineer said as he
settled down to sleep.

The grey world of the Russian steppes seemed limitless from
such a height. Limitless and empty — a land ocean into which all
petty human ventures had sunk without a trace. I could see no

towns, no roads, no signs of human habitation, only the flat expanse
of the Russian earth and the thin, twisting sprawl of great rivers,
like discarded lengths of cotton that had fallen in random, snaky
shapes, continually doubling back on themselves in great loops.
After a while the landscape beneath us changed; it became
spattered with an endless succession of perfectly symmetrical,
saucer-shaped lakes—water-logged shell holes in the no-man's-
land of an almighty Armageddon. It was a landscape such as I had
never seen before, a colander world, full of holes. At times the
lakes were so thick on the ground that the land itself seemed an
artificial intrusion, like dikes at a vast water-works. For mile
after mile these circular lakes spread beneath us and when the sun
began to sink towards the murky horizon each lake winked its
brilliant reflection back to us as we passed over. Somewhere near
that vague border that is supposed to mark where Europe ends
and Asia begins, and divides Russia from Siberia, the twilit world
seemed to erupt with a million distress signals as the red sun was
mirrored in every flashing monocle of water, big and small.

But as night covered the earth it became clear that the world of
waste and water below was not entirely devoid of life. As one by
one the glowing lakes were extinguished by the encroaching
darkness, minute sparks of flame were kindled along their banks
and the smoke from these fires rose towards us in vertical columns
until, at a certain height, they were caught by an upper wind-
stream and blown straight and far across the dusky woods and
plains like smoke from a locomotive. Who owned these solitary
camp fires at the sides of round lakes many, many miles from
anywhere? What lone hunter, fugitive or prospector now sat
huddled round those burning logs in the depths of the virgin
forest and stared back at me across five miles of twilight air?
It was a strange relationship, and in some curious way I felt an
intruder on that silent communion, a five-hundred-mile-an-hour
trespasser.

It was night when we reached Omsk and the lights of the city
seemed suspended in space like fireflies in a spider's web. We
struggled with portions of incredibly muscular chicken in the

airport restaurant (furnished with rude wooden benches and graced by a solitary, sad, papier-mâché palm tree) and within half an hour we were back on the plane. Our fellow-passengers, mostly technicians and military men, appeared to have consumed a great deal of vodka in the short time at their disposal; they were as hearty as a rugger club on a Saturday night.

"Stop making violent love to the stewardess," one of them shouted as the tail of the plane jolted and swayed, "you're rocking the plane." And the stewardess, blonde and buxom and benign, smiled patiently.

"Why is there no television on board?" another shouted.

"Why don't you serve us drinks like you used to do?"

Alcoholic refreshments were now only obtainable on Aeroflot's international flights, and looking round the passengers on that flight to Irkutsk I was not surprised at the ban on drinks on internal services. I have never known a plane with such a potential for a party; each one of those beaming, bantering Russians would have gladly roistered over Siberia throughout the rest of the night.

"I want soup, beefsteak, cheese and fruit," the Bratsk engineer told the stewardess.

"You'll get nothing," she told him.

"Then I'll settle for cheese. Why don't you feed us again?"

John and I were playing chess on a board provided as part of the service when we watched in disbelief as the dawn came up barely two hours after we had seen the sun set. The horizon lightened rapidly. By the time the sun was up it was barely time for our evening dinner by our watches. And we were still over Siberia.

Not until then, I think, had I really absorbed the fact of Siberia's staggering size. The extraordinary time differential of this prodigious land relays to the brain what the eye alone can never encompass. For Siberia from end to end is, in a manner of speaking, almost as long as the complete revolution of the hands of a clock. We were passing through time meridians with monotonous regularity.

While John dozed over a chessboard whose dispositions recorded

his second defeat since the Urals and the stewardess settled down
to browse through an old copy of the *Sunday Express* I had given
her (it contained pictures of the Wynne spy trial and a headline
BRAINWASH: THE RUSSIANS SLIPPED UP, but she skipped these
and became absorbed in adverts for ladies' undies on the woman's
page) I browsed through some Russian publications which I hoped
would at least give me some notions of the land I was flying over.

"The Soviet Union," I read, "lies in two continents, occupying
half of Europe and one third of Asia. It is the biggest country in
the world. It is 8,600,000 square miles in size, or one-sixth of the
world's populated area, almost three times bigger than the United
States and fourteen times as big as Britain, France, Italy and
Spain put together. It takes an express train from Moscow more
than a week to reach Vladivostock on the Pacific Coast. It is a
distance as great as that between the Equator and the Pole. From
east to west, the Soviet Union stretches for more than 171
longitudinal degrees—almost half-way across the hemisphere.
The distance between South Turkmenia and North Siberia
exceeds 2,500 miles . . . "

Russia was big. I turned to a section on Siberia. That was big
too.

"Siberia occupies almost one-half of the entire territory of
the Soviet Union. It is nearly as large as Europe and somewhat
larger than the USA. . . "

One region alone, Yakutia, was five times the size of France,
three of its rivers were four or more times the length of Britain.
When they were having lunch in Western Siberia they were going to
bed in the east . . . I felt like adding to this catalogue of enormity.
Siberia is as long, I calculated, as three games of chess in a jet.
No one, surely, could conceive of anything greater than that.

We flew on over the great grey forest and the big, brown,
uninhabited spaces. At half-past four, local time, when my
watch told me and my body cried out to me that it was time to go
to bed, the engines throttled back and we dipped imperceptibly
towards the earth, swooping over the trees, banking over a river
the colour of lead, thundering down to a town of log cabins and

the bleak welcome of a chilly Siberian morning. We had arrived in Irkutsk. We were a little east of the longitude of Bangkok and still only half-way across Siberia.

Our arrival was, for us, a prolonged moment of sheer absurdity. What on earth were we doing *here*? A strong sense of unreality brought us near to tears of laughter as we trudged across the apron to the airport building. It didn't help much when John started to play old New Orleans blues on a tinkly piano in the Intourist waiting-room and the melancholy chords of *St Louis Blues* drifted out of the window so far from home. As he played I flicked through a selection of periodicals provided for the diversion of waiting passengers—Chinese newspapers, Mongolian hand-outs, a picture magazine called *Korea*. This last contained a cooked-up anti-capitalist diatribe which not even the Koreans could really have thought would pass muster. Beneath a photograph of a cow being craned on board a ship was a caption which read: "The Japanese imperialists plundered our livestock..." Below it was an old photo which, for all its fuzziness, clearly depicted a very early film unit shooting a scene with a hand-cranked camera; but this was not enough for the editor of *Korea*, who clearly wrote his captions before he chose his pictures; the caption to this photograph read, "The Japanese imperialists stole our land." Through the agency of a continuity-girl and a cameraman?

The sad notes of John's jazz piece clashed oddly with this oriental double-think, even more oddly with the view through the window, where grey Siberian figures, occasional Chinese, scurried from aeroplanes over the desolation of the airstrip. "St Louis woman, with her diamond rings..." Down in the airport enclosure a matron in a fur hat and padded jacket swept the paving stones between the empty, frozen flower-beds with a broom of birch twigs. Spring had not arrived in Siberia and the world looked stark.

3

Interview with a Bear

IRKUTSK was founded in 1652. For a long time it was an administrative centre for the surrounding region, a staging post for exiles and the headquarters of the gold-mining industry. Trotsky spent a period of exile here, and Admiral Kolchak, the leader of the White Army in the Civil War, was executed here in 1920. To-day it boasts a power station, a University, a branch of the Academy of Sciences of the USSR and a population of nearly 400,000. We chose, the evening after our arrival, to go to the power station.

We drove down streets of grey, turn-of-the-century façades towards the outskirts of the town. Here there were many wooden houses—detached bungalows of logs and planking—with dirt streets running between them. Some of the houses had warped and they stood, bulging and leaning, like a set for a *Hansel and Gretel* film. "It will be another fifty years before the wooden houses disappear in Russia," our driver confided to us. "They build, build, build all those big stone blocks, but still there are wooden houses. In any case, they are warmer in winter."

The river by the dam was like the source of the Nile at the Ripon Falls in Uganda (there is a big dam there, too). There were low hills rolling away from either bank, protruding rocks and a very broad river. I saw a prospect of pylons, cranes, factory chimneys, the broad grey river at twilight, the clusters of wooden cabins, the ugly rectangular blocks of flats rising out of the dirt in a sort of waste-lot litter. "You see the dam?" our driver asked. "It confirms, doesn't it, what Lenin said about our country— *Communism is Soviet power plus the electrification of our country?*"

True enough, the wires and cables carrying the new-found energy straddled the river-banks and criss-crossed the streets as thickly as washing-lines in a Naples back-street.

Our driver was born in the Crimea. His mother was shot by the Nazis and at the end of the war he had come with a friend to Siberia. He wore an air of restrained scepticism. "What do you think of Irkutsk," he asked, "now that you have seen it?" We made a polite reply, and he said, with quiet, apologetic embarrassment, "It's just like a big village, really." To which there was nothing we could say, and he added, "Last winter a bear came into the town. It was what we call a staggerer, from the way it walks. It was terribly hungry, you see, because the winter was a bad one and it couldn't get any food in the forest. It was a very desperate bear and when it came into the town they shot it. That wouldn't happen in London, I daresay."

The hooting of the Trans-Siberian Railway dominates the town like church bells on an Oxford Sunday, and the men wear their flat hats very flatly and have the granite jaws of the production posters.

. . .

The next morning, while we were still in pyjamas, our friend from Irkutsk Radio and Television arrived. "Meester Bolliss? Meester Baytling?" he enquired, his nervous face half round the door. We had both slept badly and the malapropisms did not sound so oddly in our sleepy ears as they might have done. Bullock and Battling, Bolas and Bedouin, Bongo and Boomerang, Banjo and Benzoline—really we could have been anyone at that hour of the day. I suppose our bodies were still trying to adjust their time mechanism to the leap they had made across a number of time meridians, for we both seemed pathologically tired. It had not helped that for three hours of the previous night the night porter and the concierge had kept up a loud and disturbingly romantic conversation in the hotel doorway below our window. At half-past two John had leaned out of the window and had told them, with considerable vehemence, to shut their traps. It was encouraging that in the Soviet Union a couple of bourgeois imperialists like us were still allowed certain basic rights. Such as freedom of abuse.

Our man introduced himself. He said his name was Simon Dubrovnik and he was here to help us. He had helped one other Englishman that he could remember, a TV man who drank three bottles of vodka a day. "Why shouldn't he?" he said. "He was young and strong and he needed it." He asked how he could help us.

Over our breakfast we discussed the film we hoped to make.

"We would like to film around Lake Baikal," we said.

"Of course."

"We would like to photograph the seals there, for example."

"That will be difficult. No one is allowed to the northern end of the Lake. That's where the seals are."

"Well, perhaps since it's just seals we're after . . . ?"

"It will be difficult."

"Leaving out the seals," we said, "we've heard that at the *zapaviednik* . . . "

"Difficult."

" . . . at the *zapaviednik*, the game reserve, there are certain things we would like very much to see."

"The *zapaviednik* is 200 kilometres away in another territory for which you would require special visas. I'm afraid it would be difficult."

We cracked our boiled eggs as if they were the skulls of bureaucrats. It is difficult enough to make a film of a region about which one has no prior information. It is even more difficult when the major items of one's impromptu scenario are disallowed by the only authority that can arrange them.

"What *can* we photograph at Lake Baikal?" we asked tetchily.

"There's the museum at the Baikal Research Institute," Dubrovnik said. "It contains many interesting exhibits."

"But is that all?"

"Of course not. Lake Baikal is part of our great natural heritage. It is a place of great beauty, a great tourist attraction. We have a wonderful sanatorium there for our workers. There are many things you can photograph."

"Supposing," we suggested, "that we took a boat out on to the lake and filmed from that . . . ?"

"It would be difficult. No photographs of the banks are allowed."

"You mean that though we may by all means make a film about Lake Bailak, we can't actually film the banks of the lake? That only leaves the water."

"There are plenty of things . . . "

"Supposing we borrowed an aqualung from the Research Institute (they have one, don't they?) and an underwater camera, and supposing—since we can't photograph the banks—we just confined ourselves to the water, *under* the water? Supposing we just filmed the fishes and anything else we could see *under* the water? Would that be difficult?"

Dubrovnik looked at us and smiled happily. "No," he said, "it would not be difficult. It would be impossible."

By the time toast came we had reached some kind of an impasse. My worst fears seemed to be realised. I had come to Russia with hopes of making a film of an eternal, natural Russia remote from the world of dialectic and ideological argument. Poetry rather than propaganda was what I was after, I fondly thought—the poetry of natural things, the shapes and movements of them, of the passing seasons, the ice breaking, the spring flowers blooming, the leaves falling, Russia as it had always been. But even such harmless lyricism was to be denied me. Even the seals, fishes, bears and shores of Baikal were on the proscribed list. Doom, I thought, doom.

"If I can help in any other way," Dubrovnik was saying, "you have only to let me know. In the meantime, I have arranged for you to visit the aluminium refining plant and the Irkutsk hydro-electric station . . . "

"But . . . "

" . . . and tomorrow, perhaps, we can pay a short visit to Baikal."

. . .

Irkutsk is little more than a hundred miles from the Mongolian border; between the two interposes the great sweep of Lake

Baikal, whose westernmost tip is barely forty miles from the city. The river Angara, a tributary of one of Russia's greatest rivers, the Yenisei, flows past Irkutsk from the lake and a road runs alongside it.

We were driving along this road to Baikal in a rattling Volga car driven by a massive, likeable Ukrainian called Nikolai. It was a grey day and the road was winter-scarred, bumpy and full of potholes. The winter, which had been the worst in living memory, had torn at the Siberian earth and I saw the exposed flesh of the land, the wounds in the clay, the erosions and the weather-gouged ditches.

The great Siberian taiga, which provides eighty per cent of the Soviet Union's timber, reaches from far in the north right down to the shores of Baikal, and the road to the lake goes straight through it, cut like a Roman road for the convenience of legion-aries. The sombre green conifers—larches, firs, pines and cedars—and the silver birches not yet in leaf crowded down to the side of the road, and through the trees I sometimes caught glimpses of the Angara whose waters, when the sun was not shin-ing, were dark and gloomy. Oppressive, heavily-timbered hills fell straight into the river on the other side, but on our side there were occasional villages of wooden houses lining wide earthen streets where little children played in thigh-length woollen stockings and fur hats and peasant women were fetching water.

After an hour we came out of the trees and down to the edge of the lake. Many miles away we could see, across the long stretch of water, the snow-capped Sayan mountains. A cold wind blew off the lake but the water was calm.

Baikal, which comes from the Turkish *Bai-kul*, meaning "Holy Sea", has been described as one of the great scenic miracles of all Siberia, and the Russians are very proud of it. It is certainly a most remarkable part of the earth's surface. We learnt a lot about it that morning.

We learnt, for example, that it was the deepest lake in the world. It had been formed as the result of a fissure in the earth's crust caused by an earthquake (there are earth tremors still in the area) and latest soundings have recorded a maximum depth of 6,200 feet. It is not the largest lake in the world, Lake Victoria in East Africa is. But, though it covers a smaller area than Lake Victoria, it contains more water.

"If all the 336 rivers flowing into Baikal stopped flowing," our informant at the Baikal Research Institute told us, "and only the Angara, the lake's only effluent, was left, the lake would take 400 years to empty. In fact, I would go so far as to say that ten per cent of all the world's fresh water is contained in Baikal. And it is very fresh. If I throw a one-kopek piece into the water you can still see it forty metres down. It is so fresh that you can put it straight into accumulators. And yet—ours is such a mysterious lake—it contains salt-water fish. Salt-water fish in a lake that is 2,000 miles from the sea!"

It was certainly a very mysterious lake. It was the size of Switzerland, and in winter all of it froze solid to a depth of four feet—so solid that a good, hard road could be laid across it till the thaw. During the winter the ice contracts and expands and is forced upwards in great pressure waves; when it cracks in the spring and the floes grind against each other the noise is terrifying. Even in summer the water is cold and at a depth of 800 feet the phenomenon known as homothermia takes place—the water remains permanently at a temperature of 38° F. Great storms trouble the surface of Baikal, storms terrible enough to sink steamships; waves ten feet high ride beneath the ice in winter, and in summer a great rolling surf reaches up the shore. The noise of the surf can be heard many miles away on the mountains. But there are long periods of calm in winter and spring, days of deep blue skies and a miraculous purity of light.

"It is such a beautiful place," the biologist whose task it was to show us round the Research Station was saying to us, "I wouldn't like to leave. And so very interesting. In a way it is a unique natural laboratory. 1,800 sorts of plants and animals live in it and more than a thousand of them are found nowhere else in the world. Take the strange *golomyanka*, for example. There is a specimen of it here, can you see? Now this fish is a very odd fish, a spider fish. It has no scales. It is quite bald. And it has no colour, just a dead waxy white. Some of them are even partly transparent, and they are composed of thirty per cent pure fat. A thirty per cent fat fish! It lives at incredible depths—below 300 metres certainly. An ordinary fish cannot survive below 200 metres, and a steel vacuum tube is crushed at 300 metres. But this fish lives happily in a pressure equal to fifty atmospheres. And that is not all. This fish is viviparous. That is to say, it gives birth to its fry like a mammal. 2,000 or 3,000 babies at a time. What a fish . . . !"

The road ended a mile or two beyond the Institute and there was a small village here built entirely of wood, with a little restaurant that was closed for repairs and a few vessels tied up at the jetty. The houses were all painted in bright colours; each house was a different colour and trim and shiny as a royal barge. It wasn't long before I discovered why. Scrawled in big red letters on a wall were the words "VIVA CUBA!" On another I read "CASTRO DA, YANKEE NYET!" *He* had been here before us. We were following in his steps on what was clearly the grand tour of Siberia.

.   .   .

A Russian in a brown corduroy suit joined us at dinner that evening and it wasn't long before we were involved in conversation with him. It turned out that he was an electrical mechanic at the Irkutsk hydro-electric station. He had been born in Tula forty-three years ago and had been married for twenty-two years and had a daughter aged fourteen. He had joined the Red Army in 1938, had fought throughout the war and had met up with the American and British soldiers in Berlin. "I personally liked them," he said. "If nations were like individuals, there would be peace. Here in the Soviet Union there are all races—look around this restaurant . . . " Certainly the restaurant had a very mixed clientele, containing Russians and Mongolians (or, at least, Mongolian-*looking* people) in about equal proportions. He told us he earned 140 roubles a month, of which only six roubles went on the rent of a three-roomed flat with television, radio and sewing-machine thrown in. He worked four days on and four days off. He should work seven hours a day for six days a week, but by private arrangement with his mates he worked twelve hours a day during his four days on. "What exactly do you do at the power-station?" we asked him. "Nothing," he said, "it is fully automatic. I read books in front of dials all day. At the moment I am reading *The Mystery of the White Spot*. It's a thriller about two British spies—if you'll pardon me mentioning it—who are with a party of Russian geologists in the Siberian taiga. The Russian chief's assistant is also a spy and on the boat the chief's daughter breaks a leg and they all go into the taiga for ten years and roam about in animal skins . . . "

"Oh yes?" we said.

"What do you think of Castro?" our friend asked as he lowered his head almost into his soup-plate. "He has just visited my power station, you know. He came from a rich family, a capitalist family. Like Lenin. Lenin's brother was shot for trying to assassinate the Tsar. Have you seen his tomb? Lenin's, I mean, not his brother's?"

He was very affable. He seemed neither surprised nor disturbed that we were from England and spoke more freely than anyone I had met in Moscow under similar circumstances. We talked about Siberian animals, Lake Baikal, the River Angara and the fish you could catch in it, the weather and American cosmonauts. He spoke with knowledge and intelligence, and though he had immense pride in the achievements of Communism he was not blind to its shortcomings. "I know, of course, America is more advanced in many ways. I know in England a worker can possibly buy a car and I can't. But you wait. Just you see. Take the country round here. In Tsarist times there was nothing. Now . . . " (he waved his arm around the room) "now Irkutsk is a wonderful place. Roads . . . there are roads all over the Soviet Union. Wonderful roads. And a car isn't necessary. All I need for my family is for them to be fed, clothed and shod. Nothing else. But excuse me even Lenin had to eat."

He was in a hurry; his wife would scold him if he was late home. He drained his vodka, paid his bill, left a one-kopek tip, said it was nice meeting us, and departed. A good, straight, honest Russian worker, no doctrinaire side, no cant, no table-thumping and with none of the belligerent insecurity and inverted snobbery of intellect of many of his British counterparts.

. . .

It wouldn't be so bad, living in Irkutsk. I'd have a little plot, just a garden perhaps, with a whitewashed fence of larch palings, and a little wooden house (they're better to look at than live in, they say) with carved wooden shutters which I would paint blue or red according to which colour paint I could get in the co-operative, and I'd put geraniums in the window in the spring-time, just like everyone else, and chop wood in the autumn so that I could keep warm in the winter, and in the winter I'd light a stove and when it was hot and roaring I'd sit by it and read the short stories of Turgenev, in the original, and those of Chekhov and all the other books I had meant one day to read but never quite got round to; and I'd look out of the window and see the thick flakes of snow drifting past, sifting down and gathering in the corners of the window-pane till the window was a porthole, and I'd read about Napoleon's retreat from Moscow (what a victory that was!) in *War and Peace*, which I am sure would keep me occupied till the thaw, assuming I wasn't having to work out ways of increasing production in the local *kombinat*. Oh, there's many ways I could enjoy myself in Irkutsk. I could go to the theatre, the cinema, the art gallery, the concert hall; eat black-cock and wild duck in the summer and autumn; pick mushrooms and berries, catch the big fine fish of Siberia, and grow cabbages the size of barrels in the fertile soil of the south. Oh yes, I could bear it here, if I had to. I think, providing *they* left me alone.

. . .

I saw him loom in the open doorway of the restaurant like a bristling and bewildered bear that had trundled in from the forest. The doorman tried to make him take off the cloth cap that was pulled over his skull as tightly as a wig, but he was brushed aside and the bear swayed forward to survey the company and select his prey. Please God, I said, averting my eyes and hiding behind my glass of beer, not us. But he had seen us, alien and strange in that homogeneous company of boozing, check-shirted Russians, and he lumbered forward, picking his way through the copses of tables, his felt boots stiffly hacking through the undergrowth of pro- truding legs, till he towered over us and roared politely, "Is anyone sitting in this chair?" No, we said, nobody; and he subsided opposite us with a sigh, removed his cap, and stared. He stared fixedly through his oriental slit-eyes, not malevolently but with a consuming curiosity, and at length an inscrutable smile lit his massive face and he said suddenly: "Who the hell are you?"

"We are correspondents," John replied. He looked like a shifty Goldilocks apprehended with a mouthful of porridge.

"From?"

"Guess." It was our favourite game.

There was a long pause. The bear sat back in his chair and stared. But he did not see us, I'm sure. Somewhere in the foggy recesses of his brain a map appeared, an amorphous shape with vaporous edges full of blank spaces that represented Europe; names learned from the radio were glimpsed with difficulty through the clouds of confusion; pretty propaganda pictures of freedom-loving peoples were laboriously assembled like a jig- saw puzzle in his rustic head. Then there was a gleam of triumph and he leaned forward and confidently whispered, "You are from Czecho-Slovakia."

"Wrong," we said. We were tired; we had eaten our meal and drunk our beer; we didn't want to play this game any more.

"From Lithuania, then? Or Bulgaria? No? You are from . . . ?"

"We are from England," we told him.

"From *England*?" Disbelief gave way to a cunning pride. He leaned forward again. "I have a brother," he said, "and he has seen them. He has seen them all pointing towards your country. England is a very small country."

"Seen what?" we asked.

"I cannot say. But my brother has seen them, he told me so.

England is a very small country. If they land on England—bang!
No more England. Just dust. Russia is a very big country with
many rockets trained on England. I cannot tell you more, it is a
secret. Why are you here?"

"We are correspondents. We have come to see the achievements
of the Russian people."

"And the achievements of the Buryat people? I am a Buryat,
I come from the southern shores of Baikal. To-day I have come
200 kilometres on—" he paused dramatically, timing his sentence
to create suspense, to get the best effect from what he was going
to say—"on my motor-bike."

We showed no astonishment, no envy. "You understand," he
said, "*my* motor-bike, 200 kilometres. I am a Mongol. Not a
Mongol but a Buryat. The Buryats are the forebears of the
Mongols. Also of the Chinese. Big people. We have done
wonderful things."

"Are there many bears where you live?" we asked him.

"Of course, many. They attack people. You can't go around
without a gun."

"Why do they attack people?"

"Because they are wild animals. That is why they are called
wild animals."

We asked him if he knew of a strange white fish, blind and
without scales, which lived deep in the waters of Baikal and gave
birth to fishes like babies. He listened, apparently with rapt
attention, his large, full, seemingly boneless face registering
nothing but a sphinx-like interest, but, as soon as we had finished
he launched into an irrelevant tirade. He had been preparing it
while we were asking our question.

"I tell you," he said passionately, "in Tsarist times the
Buryats were held for nothing. But now under the Soviet Government all races are equal. Now I can eat in the best hotel in Irkutsk
and talk to two English correspondents. The Soviet system, you
understand, is the best system."

By way of demonstration, he beckoned a Russian waitress and
gave an order for a bottle of "Madeira" wine, three bottles of

beer and three full meals. We protested that we had already
eaten and that we could not expect him to buy so much drink
for us. But he would not listen. The bear had come in from the
forest with a wallet full of roubles; he was going to paint the
place red if it bankrupted him—and what more propitious start
for such an historic visit than the company of two English
correspondents? Already an ancestral pride was asserting itself.

"You must come to my village. We will kill a ram for you in
the Buryat manner. There will be a mound of meat as high as
this," and he raised his arm above his head, "and we will have a
big party. We will get drunk together in the Buryat manner. But
to-day I am in town. We will drink as best we can."

The bottles came, and he opened them all and poured out three
full tumblers of wine.

"My friends," he said, "there must be no war. Think of the
women and children. What have the English done to the Buryats?
Or the Buryats to the English? I like the English. Do you like
the Buryats? Of course you do." He peered at us through the two
little twinkling gashes in his wind-tanned head. "Think of the
rockets."

He stood, clutching his glass. "Now," he said, "we must
have a toast." We stood, too, remembering sadly that we had
been through all this many times before, and we clinked our
glasses together as he said, with deep emotion, exactly what he
had been taught to say and what we knew he would say.

"To peace and friendship."

Solemnly we drained our glasses, regretfully we chased the
wine with a glass of beer. But we didn't have time to sit down.
Our glasses were filled again, and again we clinked them together.

"To the friendship of our two nations, the Buryats and the
English."

Again the force-feed of alcohol, the brutal slaughter of what
might have been a good bottle of wine if only we had had the
chance to taste it. Our companion sat down heavily; already he
was quite drunk.

I stood and said simply, "Here's to us."

"What did he say?" the bear asked John.

"He said, 'I give you a solemn toast to the peaceful amity of all nations and to the peaceful economic growth of the Soviet Union and Great Britain so that all may prosper in glorious times ahead.'"

Our friend beamed, drank and leaned forward.

"I am a tractor-driver. Not a tractor-driver but an engineer. I am, in my way, quite a big bossman. I have *Russians* working under me! I also study. I work in the day and in the evenings I study."

"What do you study?" John asked.

There was a long pause from the bear, a drawing up of himself before the pronouncing of a solemn and confidential judgement.

"That," he said, "is a secret."

We looked at him blankly.

"How can I tell you anything when you don't publish the truth? Do you publish the truth in England?"

The confidence of his own knowledge and opinions wavered at the boundary of light and darkness. To him we were something from Mars.

"What is it like in England?" he asked, and he added, "Why should I not like the English? In the war they were our friends. There must never be another war. Think of the rockets. Think of the women and children."

The hurly-burly of his thoughts clouded his brow. The mention of war had set up a chain of ideas in his brain and under the immediate influence of the "Madeira" he began to return to the spirit of his ancestors.

"No more war," he said.

"No," we agreed.

"I was in the last war." (Proudly.)

"Yes?"

"I took part in the storming of Berlin. And I fought in Manchuria against the Japanese. Those were times! The Japanese were formidable but thirty of us in the night—Buryats like me—could kill a whole battalion of them."

He leaned forward.

"Once —" he said.

"Yes?"

" —I saw seven Japs on the skyline. So I aimed my machine gun . . . "

"And then?"

"And then —"

We waited expectantly.

"*Dadadadadadadada!*" His fingers pulled an imaginary trigger and his fists shook with the imaginary recoil of his imaginary weapon. Faces peered round anxiously from neighbouring tables at the exuberant sounds of battle. The bear clutched his bullet-torn chest, seized his throat in an agony of death and screamed, "*Aaaaaaah!*"

"Dead," he said. "All of them."

"Well done."

"That's not all. In the dead of night we would creep up to them. We would have knives in our hands and we would creep up so quietly they didn't hear us. And then . . . "

Slowly his hand, clutching the imaginary dagger, rose above his head.

"*Aaaaaaa!*"

The terrible sound flew round the room. His hand rose and fell as if he were mashing potatoes. Everywhere peace-loving citizens were staring at us in mesmerised horror, mouths open, knives and forks arrested in mid-course. We bowed low over our glasses of beer.

"Done for," the bear said happily. "Hundreds of them."

"Eat your Solyanka," John said. "Before it gets cold. There's a good chap."

"Those were times," the bear said. "Now I am forty. I have a daughter of eighteen and another who's sixteen. I have a *Russian* wife!"

He sat back to watch the impact of that lie register on our faces and, satisfied with our reaction, continued with an even bigger one.

"She is a doctor."

Secretly John had arranged with the waitress to pay part of the bill. Now she brought the rest of it and the bear, with pride and satisfaction, paid it.

"If you had come to my village," he said amiably as he collided with the doorpost on his way out, "we would have killed a ram . . ."

.   .   .

People seem to go to Irkutsk for the sole purpose of going on somewhere else. It is a pleasant enough city, as provincial cities go—an elderly doyen haunted with memories, still keeping up a reserved area of culture and learning in the barbarian outback—but people tend to hurry on after a day or two, precipitated in all directions by train or aeroplane. For Irkutsk, in a sense, is a great clearing house of the Siberian hinterland, the air junction where you catch your connection to the endless wilds of the north. It is here, too, that you catch the plane to Peking, for Irkutsk is the stepping-stone between those two great promontories of the Marxist world, Russia and China. When I was there, shortly before the Sino-Soviet rift widened to a gulf, you could see commuting delegations of impeccably dressed Chinese, shiny briefcases in hand, and you could order such exotic refreshments as *trepang* (in appearance and texture a most repulsive delicacy which I think, on close analysis, may have been canned sea-horse) and Red Chinese Vermouth, made, according to the label, by the "Chang Yu Pioneer Bottling Co. of Hankow (Gold Medal, Paris, 1915)".

John and I were no different from the other transitory visitors to Irkutsk. We had arrived there in order to pass on. Our itinerary had been approved in Moscow and after a few days we prepared to set out on the first stage of it. Our route lay northwards to a place called Bratsk, 300 miles away. The name meant nothing to us, it was just a destination on an air-ticket. All we had been told was that it was on the Angara river and that they were building a dam there that was worth seeing.

Thus it was that, in befitting ignorance, we set off for the interior of Siberia.

4

Bratsk

IT was never easy to travel in Siberia in the old days. The country was too huge and too hard. The climate was so inclement and the outposts and settlements were so widely scattered that a journey was neither comfortable nor swift. You set out only with very good reason.

I have read that before the construction of the Trans-Siberian Railway it could take a year to cross the length of Siberia. I can well believe it. From the Ural Mountains in the west to the Pacific Ocean in the east is a distance of well over 3,000 miles, and there is no natural route. To traverse such a prodigious land you would have to pass through the largest forest on earth and cross the greatest rivers of the old World; you would have to negotiate swamps and steppes and mountains and if you went north beyond the northernmost fringes of the forest there would be the bleak, permanently frozen wastes of the tundra stretching featureless before you. Every journey was an expedition. You went armed, in company, with ample provisions; you braved wild animals, bandits, disasters; you endured the privations of the stinking rest-houses on your route, the cold of winter, the deep mud of spring, the heat, dust and mosquitoes of summer; and you arrived, in all probability, at a miserable outpost or uncouth town on the backside of the civilised world. It is hardly surprising that in those days most travellers in Siberia were involuntary ones — exiles, convicts, militiamen and those who couldn't make a go of it back in the west.

The earliest travellers had used the great rivers as a way of access to the interior of Siberia. From the settlements they had founded on the river banks they radiated into the surrounding territories—on horseback in summer, by sledge in winter. There were no roads then and there are precious few now; for several centuries the frozen rivers were the best highways Siberia had and if you were lucky you might make a hundred miles a day in post-chaise sledge with a fur-lined cab and a little charcoal stove.

The Trans-Siberian Railway changed all that—at least for those wishing to make the main, direct west-east crossing. True, it wasn't properly completed until 1917, the year of the Revolution, and so it benefited the Soviets more than it ever benefited the Tsars. But for the last years of the old era travellers could use the greater part of the line and travel in comfort across the vastnesses, in a train that boasted bathrooms, music salons, a complete Russian Orthodox Church, bedroom suites and lounges where you could gamble at card tables over a genuine Scotch and soda. At first the crossing took thirty-eight days—slow by present-day times but fast indeed compared with previous standards. For before the railway was built it was quicker to travel from Vladivostock to Moscow by way of San Francisco, New York, Hamburg and St Petersburg, and those who could afford it went in this way. Now it takes nine days to cover the 5,787 miles of the overland journey.

But though, in a broad sense, the Trans-Siberian opened up Siberia, it wasn't much help if your destination lay somewhere many hundreds of miles away from it in the depths of the forest or tundra. Even now the railway system of Siberia, apart from the single broad track across it, is hopelessly inadequate; and metalled trunk roads are rare. The interior of this gigantic land would still be a difficult and exclusive morass if it were not for the advent of another technological invention—the aeroplane.

It is the aeroplane and its versatile offspring, the helicopter, that have subdued Siberia. Nowhere is inaccessible any longer; no rock rich in mineral ores can guard its treasures any more behind a zariba of fir forests and a complex of riverine defences; no bog can consider itself safe from the intrusion of the survey team; no remote hamlet of log huts, no collection of tents of reindeer skin

in the wastes of the furthest peninsula can neglect its daily delivery of *Pravda* and the latest Party line. Siberia has been dimini-
shed, if not yet tamed. Every settlement, mine and development
project in the outback has its clearing in the taiga, its dirt strip
of beaten earth and its little posse of biplanes and helicopters.
The silent wastes are noisy now with the drone of the regular
mail plane, the judder-judder of rotor-blades; the bears, they say,
are having to take sleeping-pills.

This is splendid, of course, for Siberians; they travel by plane
because it is the only sensible way to travel, because it is cheap,
quick and comfortable. But, for a traveller like myself, this
preponderance of air travel was a continual source of frustration.
In a sense, I was traversing Siberia by avoiding it. Between me
and the mysteries of this land on such journeys there was always
a distance of several thousand feet. I felt cheated.

I felt cheated when we went to Bratsk in this way, in a "wild"
plane with broken seat-belts and a dented wing. The plane
looked exactly like a Dakota and was evidently of some antiquity.
It inspired no confidence in us whatever and we peered through
the porthole at the engines with considerable intensity as the
plane lumbered into the air and growled across the forest towards
the north.

We struggled up to 6,000 feet and began to pitch and bump
badly. A small child was suddenly sick over its mother but
didn't utter a murmur; no one seemed to care and I got up and
gave the mother a paper bag for her child to be ill in. Dubrovnik
leaned forward and tapped John on the shoulder. John was asleep
but pretended not to be.

"Look at the taiga," Dubrovnik said.

"*Da*," John said, "I am."

"It's big, isn't it?"

"Yes, big."

"Are you looking?"

"Yes."

"Have you ever seen so many trees?"

"Never."

"Don't you find it impressive?"

"Yes."

"Really?"

"Absolutely extraordinary," John said, and fell again into a defensive sleep.

Dubrovnik sat back in his seat. "Taiga," I heard him croon. "Oh, the taiga . . ."

The taiga was big. It was also on fire. Great plumes of smoke billowed from its grey depths, great barbs of flame leapt and flickered on the edge of a charred and blackened area. It was strange to see the forest on fire and the rivers that twisted through it still white with ice in the shallows. The land below had no rest from the savagery of the seasons.

After an hour and a half we came in low and banked steeply. Suddenly I had a glimpse of a river gorge and a great wall of concrete and then we were plummeting into the forest. I heard the pilot throttle back the engines and knew instinctively, though I am no pilot, that we were still too high. There was a pause and then we slammed into the red earth of the airstrip. We bounced once and fell again heavily to the ground. We had been deposited at Bratsk.

It was not long before we realised that we had come to a place that was very different indeed from any we had been to so far. The airfield hacked out of the trees, the broad dirt road cut like an autobahn through the ageless forest, the power trucks passing backwards and forwards like ants, the water lorries spraying the roads with powerful jets to settle the dust, the view of the great dammed river and above it the spacious township of splendid two-storeyed houses of new wood—all proclaimed something new and wondrous and exciting. Here man was challenging the primeval earth. With all the resources of one of the greatest nations in history concentrated like a sunbeam through a magnifying glass on this one spot in the midst of the wild taiga, nature was being transformed, moulded into the shape of a dream, bent to the service of man. The coniferous trees that had sprouted, grown and withered unchallenged since the Ice Age stood tall and silent at the edge of the clearings as if in mourning. The river, checked for the first time since the world began, spilled in frustration over the surrounding countryside. Man was king.

The "hotel" to which we were driven from the airfield turned out to be a flat on the top floor of a new wooden house. It had two rooms, a kitchen, bathroom and lavatory. The outside door, which closed itself on a powerful spring, was insulated against the cold with a thick felt padding covered in leather; central heating warmed the interior. The flat had a large radio set on which, if we wished, we could listen to the BBC news; and a telephone with which we could telephone London. The windows opened on to a screen of tall cedars, beneath which clustered a village of simple wooden shacks where the dam workers had lived in the early days of the construction. Beyond the shacks I could see the Angara river and the great artificial lake formed by the dam. It wasn't until I saw an oil tanker float into view, breasting the waves of this new man-made inland sea, that I fully appreciated the magnitude of the operations at Bratsk. Then I saw the dam.

It was on the left and partly obscured by the trees in the foreground. It was late evening now and getting dark. Even so, the glimpse was staggering. It was like seeing a mountain when one expected a tumulus. Its massive flanks strode the river, reared beyond the banks like a towering monument to the most grandiose visions of the human species. Looking at it then in the gathering dusk, looming grey and monstrously large between the trees, I found myself being overcome by a curious unease, an insidious feeling of insignificance. I began to feel oddly puny, useless and guilty at the futility of my own aspirations and petty achievements by comparison with the splendour of this dam. What I had done in my whole life, I thought then, was nothing compared with the riveting of one bolt, the casting of one concrete pile at Bratsk; in contrast with this commemoration of selfless communal endeavour my own existence was both selfish and mercenary.

Such thoughts, of course, were absurd; but they were very real at the time. Even then, though, I recognised their true nature.

For I realised that I was expecting from Bratsk the peacetime equivalent of the moral climate of war. I was hoping that what I had been looking for in the Soviet Union and not yet found I might, if I were to find it at all, find here.

.   .   .

My experience of Russia up to the moment I set foot on the raw red earth of Bratsk had been disappointing. I do not think the reason can be found in any abstract discussion of the relative merits of Communism or capitalism or in the bandying of statistics which might or might not prove something or nothing. At the risk of sounding trite, I would agree that Soviet achievements since the Revolution have been staggering and that their achievements will, in all probability, be no less remarkable in the future. If my experience of the Soviet Union had been confined to a visit to a model factory, a successful collective farm, *Swan Lake* at the Bolshoi, a tour of the Kremlin, a perusal of *Pravda* and a discussion of the Seven Year Plan with a Party member, I am sure I would have doffed my cap long ago. No, the problem was simpler, more personal. It was just that I didn't like living in the Soviet Union.

Why? A hundred reasons rush to my mind. It is difficult to find a single common denominator among them. Some of them even appear ridiculously superficial. Take, for example, pubs. I like pubs, I like to drink in them, I like to talk to people in them, I like looking at people in them. There were none in Moscow. It was not a terribly important lack. There were none in New York either. It was just that, in Moscow, there was nothing else. I remember Vadim saying, "There aren't many places where you can live it up here, but there are some." I never found them. I never found anywhere, except in the formal encounter at the restaurant table, where I could meet a Russian man or woman casually and informally and we could let our hair down and talk about anything under the sun and not fear the consequences of anything we said. Oh, you could meet the Russians all right, but not in the way I was accustomed to meet people, not in the way it was right and natural to meet people. You could meet Russians over the office table, at the factory bench, beside the *kolkhoz* tractor. Your conversation would be limited to the formula question and answer, the conventional State-approved statement. You would learn what next year's production figures would be, you might even have a drink to the accompaniment of some suitable toast, you would leave possibly with a bunch of flowers in your arms, handshakes and smiles all round. Wonderful people, so earnest, so eager, so friendly. But you would know, afterwards, that you had been soft-soaped. Your encounter was about as fruitless as a love affair conducted through the intermediary of the Marriage Guidance Bureau. You had been censored.

In the end you gave up hoping to meet a Russian on the same terms as you would hope to meet a Frenchman or a Ghanaian or a Burmese. In the end you gave up inviting them to lunch next day or asking them back to your room for a drink and a chat. They were afraid to, and in the end you were afraid, too. If the trial of Penkowski served one purpose, it was to warn Russians to keep clear of westerners with their seductive riches, their heretical, corrupting small-talk, their ill-gotten glamour; and more than one foreigner has been clapped in gaol for asking too many innocent questions. The few—the happy, free, doomed few— who were desperate enough or foolish enough to choose our company for its own sake, say what they wanted and do as they liked, were a disavowed minority, untypical, un-Soviet. For the rest, it was like talking to a Jesuit with his God leaning over his shoulder. He said his unquestioning, unquestionable piece, and moved on. You learnt nothing that way.

It was surprising, really, how little you did learn that you couldn't have found out from a Soviet newspaper or hand-out. Russia, in a sense, was one big PR job. The warm handshakes, the ingratiating bland smile, the juggle of facts and figures, the glossy little brochure and the so-called "typical" showpiece—these fix the faithless, keep the capitalist wolf from the socialist door. So your tour of the country was strictly conducted and you shuffled—bored, tired and confused—from one factory to another and in and out of State farms, opera houses, higher educational institutes, research institutes, clinics, pioneer camps, museums, sanatoria, aluminium plants, workers' clubs and the Intourist hotels. Everywhere, really, except inside an ordinary Russian's home. It was surprising, after being shown so much, how little you had learned.

For the present hardly existed except in relation to the past and the future. "Oh, you should have seen it in Tsarist times!" was the cry. "Oh, but you should see it next year." Or the year after that, or the year after that. Any question, any doubt or criticism about Russia to-day was expertly parried or ducked. "It is better than it was," you would be told. "It will be better than it is." The present was what you wanted it to be, what you thought it ought to be; rarely what it actually was; like molten lead, it was so fluid you could cast it in any mould. And they frequently did. So successfully that I had to resort, when opportunity offered, to going to the small reading-room in the British Embassy in Moscow in order to read back numbers of *The Times* and find out what really was happening. It was never quite clear from the *Daily Worker*, the only British newspaper publicly available in Russia.

After several weeks of that peculiarly Soviet brand of hypnotism known as (in Vadim's phrase) "showing you round", I was beginning to have DOUBTS. I began to see cracks in the Soviet edifice that I might never have noticed otherwise. For want of information on which I thought I could rely, people whom I could trust, I began to compile my own dossier and in time an uneasy conviction grew that perhaps, after all, it was all rather a fraud, a hoax which could only be kept up by letting no one into the secret. The workers' paradise, it seemed, was a delusion. And I was disappointed.

Everywhere I saw a claustrophobic conformity of thought and a deadening uniformity of things. You would encounter the same second-hand dogma and unquestioning optimism across thousands of miles, just as you would find the same identical menu card in every restaurant from Minsk to Khabarovsk (and the same

Saturday afternoon in the Siberian forest near Bratsk.

The dam at Bratsk—the biggest hydro-electric station ever built.

crockery, cutlery, cars, chandeliers, street lamps, public fountains, public parks, public statues, blocks of flats and bathroom fittings). There was drabness, boredom and ineptness. It took an hour to be served in a restaurant. There were no telephone directories you could easily lay your hands on. If you wanted to buy a tube of toothpaste you queued for half an hour to see if the shop had any and what price it was; you queued again to pay for it; and you queued a third time to get it. And when you got it, it was awful. The lavatories never stopped flushing or they wouldn't flush at all. The finishing of buildings and manufactured goods was often appalling—doors wouldn't shut, walls were cracked, tiles were stuck on like a crude attempt at an abstract collage. You waited twenty minutes for a lift in the Ukraine Hotel in Moscow. If you found you'd left something in your room on the twenty-fifth floor after you'd got to the ground floor, you could spend another forty minutes going up and down again. Aeroplanes regularly didn't take off on time—if you arrived an hour late for a flight you could still catch it. If you had a flat and broke a window, blocked up a sink, put your foot through a floorboard, you could wait months for a repairman. I saw the manager of a city bank who had to do all his calculations on an abacus. And so on.

The argument, perhaps, smacks too much of damnation. But it was necessary to say these things in order to make the impact of Bratsk quite clear. Until then I had been neither happy nor profoundly impressed. But I am not as prejudiced as I seem. The overloaded scales will be more fairly balanced. The wrong, comrade, will be redressed.

For here was Bratsk, here was the dam.

·   ·   ·

We spent the best part of the next day going over the dam and the area around it. I am not an engineer and a great deal that I was told about the dam by the technician attached to us for the purpose went over my head. The only thing that I remember clearly was that I was frightened—physically frightened, I mean, by the noise and the size and the prodigious power being generated all around me. I do not, at the best of times, like machinery. I do not trust even a motor-car's starting handle or a simple electric hand-drill. I react with an almost animal timidity and loathing to the roar of a vacuum cleaner, and factory workshops petrify me. So it was not surprising that the turbine room of the biggest hydro-electric station in the world should startle me out of my wits. Although the dam at that time was not yet finished, a few of its monstrous turbines were already in operation. To inspect them we were invited to descend through a trap-door and down a ladder into what was, in my memory, a small black room full of roaring, whirling metal. I couldn't speak above the noise, and the vibration tingled uncomfortably through my body. Edgar Allan Poe, perhaps, would have enjoyed the place. He might have enjoyed watching John begin to step backwards into the space between the turbine and the inspection platform. Only a timely hand, it seemed, rescued him from a death by mincing, and we were both glad to leave for the comparative haven of the station control room. Here, in a gallery of half-assembled dials and jungly profusion of electricity cables, only the splutter of welding equipment and the machine-gun chatter of pneumatic drills broke the silence.

We emerged with some relief from the inferno in the bowels of this hollow edifice and went up on to the topmost deck of the dam. This carried a road, a railway and trucks for the great cranes which straddled the entire breadth of the dam and lumbered slowly up and down like herons looking for fish. An air of ordered chaos pervaded the place and I was suitably impressed. But it wasn't until I peered over the flimsy plank balustrade and stared down at the waters below that I fully appreciated the monumental proportions of the work at Bratsk. For we were more than 350 feet up—as high above the river as the dome of St Paul's. Far below, in the green waters of the Angara, I could see the trunks of uprooted trees being tossed around like matchsticks in the turbulence of a gushing sluice. The noise of the sluice, I realised, was the pervading sound of Bratsk, the background music into which all other sounds blended and were lost. We went down to the sluice later and walked out on to a wooden catwalk that ran alongside the great, white, frothing spout of ferocious water as it shot through the dam like an express train. This was the most frightening thing of all. The noise was deafening and we were drenched in fine spray; the catwalk had been partly damaged by ice and the end of it, where part of it had broken away, swayed sickeningly above the river; the plank railing wobbled, too, when you dared to rest your hand on it, and I began to doubt whether all those nails and planks were sufficient to bear our weight and the power of the river, and I saw myself falling headlong into the stormy water and being swept into the turbines and whisked into foam. What a way to go, I thought, as I scampered off the catwalk—to end up as an alternating current on the Siberian grid.

I was happier to learn more about the dam further away from its actual, disturbing presence. Later that morning we paid a visit to the Chief Engineer of the Bratsk Hydro-Electric Project, Aran Markovitch Gindin, a Jew who had been honoured with two Orders of Lenin but was not a Party member. He was a white-haired, balding, keen and energetic man in his fifties, who sat in a wooden office at a desk covered in green baize; above his head was a framed artist's impression of the finished dam, a white and elegant wall of concrete across the steep, forested banks of the river. John conducted the interview and I took some photographs. From the notes we compiled afterwards the interview went something like this—the first clear exposition we had heard of the startling promise of the new Siberia, of the Soviet dream becoming reality.

BAYLISS: We would like to ask you a few simple questions.

GINDIN: No questions are ever simple.

BAYLISS: Well, we'll do our best . . . Would you mind if we also took some photographs?

GINDIN: Of course not. I'm not a secret object, am I?

BAYLISS: The first question we would like to ask is—how did this project come about?

GINDIN: You see? You say you will ask me simple questions and

you start with a snorter like that! To answer that question I shall
have to describe the background. I don't know how much you
already know . . .

BAYLISS: Not much, I'm afraid.

GINDIN: Well, then, in the first place you have to see Bratsk not
as an isolated achievement but as part of an overall plan for the
development of Siberia. You know that before the Revolution
Siberia was nothing more than a remote, neglected colony of the
Tsars. "The biggest waste-lot in the world" —that's how one of
the Tsar's generals described it. It was a bit like America before
America was discovered, if you see what I mean. A land full of
immense riches and nobody doing anything about it. But the
Revolution changed all that. After the Revolution every effort
was made to develop Siberia and exploit its prodigious wealth . . .

BAYLISS: Could you tell us something about that?

GINDIN: About what?

BAYLISS: About the wealth of Siberia.

GINDIN: You *don't* know much, do you? All right —but I shall be
here hours at this rate. I'm a busy man. I'm building a dam . . .

BAYLISS: Just briefly.

GINDIN (*Rapidly, like a tobacco auctioneer*): Siberia has eighty per
cent of the Soviet Union's coal reserves. It has three-fifths of the
country's ore, three-quarters of its timber, plenty of zinc, copper,
tin, iron, manganese, tungsten, silver, gold, diamonds —oh,
endless mineral resources. And there's oil and natural gas as well.
It's one of the richest countries on earth. And we haven't discovered
half of it yet. But the point is, to develop these immense resources
you need power. Before you can turn Siberia into the economic
heart of the Soviet Union, tame it, exploit it, you need power to
drive machines, factories, processing plants and so on. And where
do you get power? From coal, from oil, from natural gas, from the
atom —and from water. You're with me so far?

BAYLISS: Yes. Go on.

GINDIN: Well, it so happens that Siberia also has eighty per cent
of the Soviet Union's water power. It has many great rivers. The
Ob, the Yenisei and the Lena are among the biggest in the world.

Take the Lena. It's—I don't know—about five or six times the length of your own country. It has exactly one thousand tributaries. It drains an area of one million square miles and its delta stretches across 250 miles of coastline. It's big, you see. A *big* river. That one river alone has a hydro-electric potential of twenty million kilowatts . . .

BAYLISS: I'm sorry, but it's difficult to grasp what that means.

GINDIN: Would you be very surprised if I told you it means that the Lena river is capable of producing almost as much electricity as the entire electrical output of Great Britain at the present time? Or nearly twice as much as Norway, the most highly-developed hydro-electric country in the world? And there are many rivers in addition to the Lena—Siberian water power is boundless . . . Well, the Hydroproject Design Office—that's our central planning body—has been examining all the possible sites for hydro-electric stations during the last few years and has marked them on the map. Now the work of construction has begun. On the Angara river, for example, we finished the first dam, at Irkutsk, in 1959. Bratsk is the second and will soon be finished. We have started on the third, at Ust-Ilim, and when that's built we'll move further up the river and build three more. In the end the Angara will be providing Siberia with seventy billion kilowatt hours of electricity a year. Don't ask me what that means. It's a lot.

(*Gindin is talking quietly, with the precise, clinical detachment of a technician who knows what can and cannot be done. He does not talk with the big, empty, hopeful rant of a propagandist. Listening to his cool appraisal of the things to come, we begin to catch some of the excitement of the Soviet vision, the grandiose master-plan to change the face of their part of the world. We have only to look out of the window to know that it is not idle talk.*)

So, you see, Bratsk is not an isolated achievement. It's just one part of a general plan. At the moment, yes, it's the biggest hydro-electric station in the world. Four and a half million kilowatts. But west of here, at Krasnoyarsk, on the Yenisei, they're building a bigger one of five million kilowatts, and soon they'll be starting on another one called Sayany-Shushenskoye, 250 miles upstream, with a capacity of more than six and a half million kilowatts.

But they are dwarfs by comparison with the Big Lena. The blue-prints for that one have been drawn up already. It's colossal, really—twenty million kilowatts, enough to supply a population of fifty million people. It will be built up in the Arctic, near the mouth of the river, and it will form a huge sea a bit bigger than Switzerland . . .

BAYLISS: Where's all this electricity going to? I mean, how is a country as thinly populated as Siberia going to make use of all this electricity? Most of the power stations you mention seem to be in the back of beyond.

GINDIN: There *are* such things as pylons and power lines. They'll join the stations up to the Siberian power grid and eventually to the power grid of the Soviet Union. That hasn't happened yet, but it's early days. And power stations attract industries. Here at Bratsk we're also building the biggest timber-processing plant in the world. It's a pretty obvious thing to do—we've got all this electricity and we're right in the middle of the biggest forest on earth. And there's also two aluminium plants—one's working already—planned to turn out a quarter of the world's aluminium production. The electricity will be used all right.

BAYLISS: Could you tell us more about Bratsk? How it started and so on.

GINDIN: Bratsk is quite an old name, you know. I sound like a schoolmaster, don't I? Buryat nomads used to wander round here for centuries. The first Russian explorer came here in 1631 and a little town was built here a few years later. Hunters, trappers, fishermen . . . people like that lived here. One of the Decembrist revolutionaries, Peter Mukhanov, was exiled here for ten years, and after that Bratsk became a place for exiles, forced labourers and so on. It had a bad reputation, like all Siberia. One of the first things we did when we came here was to knock down and burn any remnants of those days—the old wooden towers and the gates. We left only Peter Mukhanov's little old church . . . That was in 1955 when a vanguard of 500 volunteers arrived here. They had a tough time. In the summer the air swarms with midges and mosqui-toes; they hold up work, people can't sleep. And in the winter they only had tents to live in while they were building the permanent quarters. But they were tough, those boys. The temperature can drop to — 50° C here, but I've seen them run down to the river, break holes in the ice and bathe. Some couldn't stand it and went back to Moscow or wherever they came from — there was no compulsion to stay here. But most of them stuck it out. To-day the labour force on the dam is 5,000, and the total working population at Bratsk is over 50,000. They've come from all over the Soviet Union and I'd say that to every one who got the job three had volunteered. I mention that point specially, because I know the West often thinks Siberia is inhabited only by slaves. That's what Averell Harriman, the US Secretary of State, thought before Khrushchev sent him here to see for himself. No, the workers at Bratsk are here because they want to be here. When they've done this job, I'm quite sure most of them will want to stay on and move up-river to Ust-Ilim to start the next one. The *esprit de corps* of the work teams is fantastic. They're all young and strong. The average age of the dam-builders is under twenty-five, and a lot of them are young girls. We've been having about 300 new babies born every month here. I think that's probably a Soviet record. It makes me feel like an old man.

BAYLISS: What special difficulties did you face during the construction?

GINDIN: The weather. The long winters. The ice. The river freezes down to twelve feet. Since it flows from south to north, the ice piles up against the dam and we have to get an icebreaker to mince the ice up into little pieces so that they'll pass through the sluices. The low temperature caused all sorts of problems. For example, we couldn't keep concrete at an even consistency. So we had to heat it in winter and cool it in summer by mixing ice with it. The other problems had to do with transport and communications. We're in the heart of the taiga here, in wild and remote country. We had to get raw materials here, big machinery, cranes, dynamos. Take cement. We have used twenty million tons .of it so far — that's about 600,000 wagon-loads on a goods train stretching from Vladivostock to London. Well, we

had to get it here, so we had to build roads and railways. And we
had to build a whole new town . . . It's taken eight years so far—
it's not child's play, building a dam. But when it's all done
Bratsk will be the centre of an important industrial complex. It
will be another piece fitted into the jigsaw of the new Siberia.

·   ·   ·

The new Siberia. I remembered the engineer's words as I strode
the next day—a Sunday—through the newly-risen town. It was
not just the achievement of the dam that so impressed me, nor
what I had learnt of the plans for Russia's new world, the
Utopian materialist dream. It was something more elusive than
that, a sort of emanation.

Was it, I wondered, the individuality of the place, the attractive
detached houses of polished cedarwood and pine? They seemed so
refreshing after the monotonously dour and identical housing
projects that I had seen elsewhere—more like a new and prospering
Swedish suburb set spaciously and with grace among the trees than
the product of some central Soviet design office. Perhaps that was
it—the hint of individuality reasserting itself out here in the
Siberian wilds after the dulling conformity and sameness of
collective life elsewhere; the re-emergence of good taste and
graciousness after so much that was drab, brash or downright
ugly? For in some way Bratsk seemed to me a kind of refuge from
ideological pressures of Soviet life; secure in the middle of the
dense forest, the community seemed to blossom more freely here
and to stamp its own distinct mark on the way things were done;
the antique values of the pioneer, the old hardiness, self-reliance
and individuality of the *Sibiriak*, were perhaps taking over from
the acquired or imposed mores of Moscow.

Perhaps, too, it was the curious peacefulness of the place that I
so liked, for Bratsk—in spite of the continuous murmur of
industry coming from the dam—was blessed with an almost
monastic quiet, especially towards evening when the dying sun
would sink behind the dam and throw the great cranes into
silhouettes of delicate fretwork as intricate as filigree. Then you

would hear the rustle and sigh of the wind in the cedars along the lake and the cry of the seagulls that had come 2,000 miles from the nearest sea to feed on the torn fish that had been sucked into and spewed out of the turbines; and you would hear a guitar among the boats at the jetty and the chopping of firewood and a man ambling by playing an accordion slung round his neck, a boy alone and happy and far from home, squeezing out one of those slow, melancholy and infinitely beautiful melodies of Russia as he passed below my window to his supper; and the laughter of children, down by the creek that had crept down a valley as the dammed waters rose, fishing with sticks and hooks of bent pins and lighting fires among the bare shrubs and hummocky rough grass, a thriving generation in the old badlands.

This new-found sense of freedom was not peculiar to me. John felt the same and so, it seemed, did the young people who lived here and the Russians who visited the place. The young men and girls we had met at the open-air dance floor the previous night (so packed that we had to fight to get in and only had room to take photographs by sitting with the local brass band on a small stage) had seemed more expansive, gayer and more unreservedly delighted to meet two Englishmen than any Russians we had encountered before. They had pounced on us, chortled round us, taken us to the small room where the gramophone and amplifying equipment was (records of Parisian café music, George Brassens, Sinatra, even—could I be right?—Elvis Presley, all re-recorded on Russian discs, presumably after being lifted from Western radio pro-grammes), poured their vodka down our throats and asked if we knew Alan Sillitoe, and all the time I was conscious of this difference—that they knew no fear, they did as they wished, spoke as they wanted and were our staunch friends for as long as we stayed.

It was the same with our Russian companions at the long dining-table in the restaurant annexe to the works canteen, who spoke with us not as persons separated by a great and impassable gulf but as fellow-voyagers fetched up in the same secluded haven. There were three of them and they were journalists, reporting on Bratsk as we were. The most talkative of them was a large and impressive photographer from the Russian news magazine *Ogonyek*, a man of very considerable presence and age-less enthusiasm.

"Where are you going from here?" he asked us.

We told him.

"By the time you've finished," he said, "you'll have seen more than I have. But avoid Georgia. There's only one thing you'll do there. They'll seize you by the neck and pour drink down your throat till you're half-drowned. I ought to know . . . Are you going to Khirgizia? There's a wonderful lake there, and a hydro-electric station, too."

"He's got a one-track mind," his companion said, and winked at us.

"Or Kamchatka. Now there's a place. A great volcano and a large colony of seals—fur seals. The Japanese used to poach them from the off-shore islands and when they couldn't do that any more they poured oil all over the beaches. When I was there I had to crawl along on my belly so that the seals would think I was one of them. But a great big bull spotted me and charged after me—he thought I was after one of his wives. I got some good shots, though. Anyway, here's to the success of both our ventures—and I must say I wish I was doing what you're doing."

Our conversation turned to other places. The journalists were well travelled. The photographer alone had been to South America, China, and India. "He did a whole course in English before he went and he doesn't speak a word," one of his companions remarked. "It wouldn't have done me any good," the photo-grapher said. "The Indians couldn't understand our interpreter, but they got on fine with one of our party who spoke perfect pidgin." He had been to England in 1956, covering the visit of Khrushchev and Bulganin, and he had been impressed, he said, by Madame Tussaud's, the gas-lamps along Millionaires' Row, the whores in the Bayswater Road, Barker's department store in Kensington High Street ("for millionaires only, surely?"), the

The new generation of Siberia. Top left—young volunteers at Bratsk. Top right—
time off for new-found glamour. Bottom—girl workers at the Bratsk dam above
a banner proclaiming the new Soviet faith. It reads: "Long live Communism,
which is establishing in the world Peace, Work, Freedom, Equality, the Brother-
hood and Happiness of all peoples".

ДА ЗДРАВСТВУЕТ КОММУНИЗМ, УТВЕРЖДАЮЩИЙ НА ЗЕМЛЕ МИР, ТРУД,
СВОБОДУ, РАВЕНСТВО, БРАТСТВО И СЧАСТЬЕ ВСЕХ НАРОДОВ!

The old generation of Siberia.   Top left—a former inmate of a slave labour camp. Top right—a pre-Revolutionary immigrant. Bottom—the old faith still manages to survive. A Churchman is greeted by the faithful.

Scene during an ordination service in Irkutsk Cathedral conducted
by the Archbishop of Siberia and the North.

The children of Russia.

dense traffic in the narrow streets, the beauty of Edinburgh, the sands of Littlehampton, the film *Genevieve*, the unruly under-graduates of Oxford (I remembered the visit well, we threw firecrackers behind Khrushchev and sang *Poor Old Joe* on the Town Hall steps), the friendliness of the English and the children asking for Russian match-boxes. "Everyone was very friendly and obliging," he said. "I liked England. I'd like to go again. But it's just as nice to meet two young Englishmen in the middle of Siberia."

After the journalists had gone, we stayed on into the late hours of the still Siberian night, talking with unaccustomed frankness to our Bratsk guide. He was a willowy, fair-haired young man of thirty-one, who looked about eighteen. He had come to Bratsk as a volunteer from Gorki, bringing his wife and small child. At first he had taught history in the local school, but when the river flooded behind the dam and his school and the entire village was drowned under 200 feet of water, he had been made a Press Officer for the hydro-electric project. It was in this capacity that he had joined up with us.

I liked this earnest, well-informed, honest young Russian. Very soon our conversation turned inevitably to the topic of Communism and capitalism and I liked the very quiet and reasonable way he argued his case and listened attentively to ours. He was, I suppose, a typical example of the young Russian intelligentsia; more than any Russian I had yet met, he searched avidly for the truth rather than platitudes and, though nothing we said could shake his resolute socialist faith, he did not, as many Russians tended to, dismiss our arguments as the ravings of delinquent bourgeois imperialists. Even so, to talk to him was sometimes like seeing a familiar face reflected back in a grotes-quely distorted glass. Korea, for example, was explained as the unprovoked attack of American imperial armies trying to bolster a corrupt and oppressive government against the will of the Korean people. The Berlin Wall was a reluctant measure taken to prevent any further mass influx of West Berliners into the free and democratic Eastern Sector. The Hungarian uprising was the work of counter-revolutionary fascist imperialist agents. He did not believe that young students and factory workers had been killed in the streets of Budapest by Russian tanks. He could not conceive that there was more than one form of colonialism and that truth was not the prerogative of one faith or government or radio station but lay, like a blinded and groping soldier, somewhere between the two firing lines.

Foreign affairs bewildered our friend, for he was perceptive enough to realise that there were things he had not heard of and could not think why. He was happier when the conversation turned to Russia, and when he talked of his motherland and of the future (always of the future) we sometimes envied him his share of that massive purposefulness, his innocent faith.

"America, I know, has the highest standard of living in the world," he said to us. "By comparison we are poor people in Russia. We do not have millionaires, who buy (like Henry Ford) gold anchors for their yachts or mink fur covers for their golf clubs. But nor do people go hungry here, or die because they cannot afford an operation, or get beaten up because their skin is the wrong colour. Our society will grow and prosper. Now it is a socialist society and in time it will be a true communist society. We will all have our equal share of that new world. Hospital porters will be equal with the surgeons, we will all have gold anchors if we want them, no one will want, no one will go to war . . . "

It seemed sad, when we abandoned our vodka and cognac in the early hours of the morning, that our friend could not stay the night on the spare bed in our flat. He asked the concierge if he could, but she would not allow it and he had to trudge a weary five miles home in the chilly darkness. Such a devoted proponent of the new society deserved better consideration.

.   .   .

The day that followed was the day of the wood-choppers' ball. We will neither of us ever forget it.

Dubrovnik had come in the morning while we were shaving and

announced that we were going to a timber camp some fifty miles to the east where they were cutting down the trees before they were engulfed by the rising waters of the lake. We had already been out on the lake in a motor-boat and seen some of the damage. There were areas in the lake where you could look down and see, deep in the water, the tops of trees that had recently drowned. It was strange because the trees looked as if they were still growing; they were green and waved in the water as they had once waved in the wind.

Dubrovnik had ordered a coach for us and we set out at nine. The road was like many I had known in Africa, with a rough dirt surface and dust flying in a great red cloud behind us; we had to hang on to our seats to prevent ourselves being thrown about. We drove on for two hours, petrified by a driver who grew gleefully more homicidal as the journey progressed. He drove like a racing driver and we were glad to get out when we reached our destination.

The timber camp was really a village of wooden houses. It was only two years old and the wood was still white and new. A motley group of lumberjacks was there to greet us and we all boarded another coach and drove for another half hour across country till we came to the work-site. Here there was a lot of felled timber that men were cutting up into logs and assembling in rafts. When the water rose the rafts would float off and be towed to the saw-mill. That way they could save a lot of the forest from destruction.

We spent the rest of the morning in and around the forest. Led by a jovial hunchback master-lumberjack (they used the English word "Master" when they addressed him) we walked into the forest, a motley and sweating company, and watched a woodman cutting down trees with a petrol-driven handsaw. He got through almost one a minute and when he had toppled a score or so a huge sixty-horse-power tractor simply towed them forcibly out of the forest to where the others were trimming them and building them into rafts.

It was hot and muggy in the forest. Mosquitoes swarmed round

us and we spent our time slapping our exposed skins and occasionally picking the cowslips that grew in profusion over the forest
floor. The cowslips had two flowers on the same stalk—one
mauve and one yellow—and we sucked the ends of them as I
vaguely remembered having done in my childhood. It was curious
how the forest evoked one's childhood and even provoked a kind
of retrogression back to it. At one time we all got excited about
a small lizard that one of the woodchoppers caught, and another
time someone said he thought he had seen a bear. There were
plenty of bears around, he said, and the year before a woman had
been mauled and killed by one. So we all played at keeping a
look-out for bears and after a while, like all children, we got bored
and hungry and walked out of the forest to lunch.

I do not remember much of that terrible lunch, that nightmare
wood-choppers' ball. Our lumberjack friends, who had never set
eyes on any Englishman before and for whom our arrival was the
event of the decade, had prepared a mountain of food for us and it
lay in steaming bowls on a trestle table at the village restaurant.
We sat down and waited politely to start. We waited for ten
minutes while the food—borshch, boeuf Stroganoff and a heap of
sardines—got cold and our empty stomachs rumbled impatiently.
Then two more lumberjacks came in carrying two large parcels full
of bottles. We must have a few toasts, they said, before we eat.

We had the few toasts.

I do not remember exactly what happened. Amnesia came bliss-
fully soon. I do remember, though, that I no longer had any
inclination to eat and that an alarm clock went off in my head and
a bomb went off in my stomach and that I was speechless. It was
my speechlessness that puzzled me. All I could do was mouth my
few incoherent syllables, for no sound issued from my vocal
chords. I realised, dimly and bemusedly, that my larynx had been
anaesthetised. I was silenced as effectively as if I had been hit by
a low punch. I tried to say "No more thank you", but nothing
happened. My mouth opened and shut like a fish. Like a fish I
swallowed the second toast.

I had always thought that this sort of thing only went on in films. In the sinister dive in down-town Hong Kong the evil Chinaman would wink once to the blonde in fishnet tights and, presto! she would be sliding a glass of Macao Highball or Kowloon Punch down the long bar-room counter. Then a gong would sound in the victim's head and he would be flat on his back on the sawdust floor and the evil Chinaman would be trussing him up and dropping him through a trapdoor to the sharks.

No, it wasn't just in films, it was happening here, in a rude log cabin in the Bratsk taiga, and there was nothing we could do about it. We were trapped, not by any sinister oriental plot but by the simple laws of hospitality. We could not refuse the proffered potion, the clear, disgusting concoction known as Siberian Spirit, and slowly and painfully we passed into a state of complete intoxication.

The drink was fire. It was ninety per cent pure spirit and we had to drink it by the tumbler-full. Worse, we had to drink it down in one. Dubrovnik was watching to see that we did.

"To peace and friendship," our host, the Assistant Director of the timber camp, said. We drained the glass dry and chased it as quickly as we could with another tumbler containing water. I turned, gasping for breath, my eyes watering as if I'd been punched on the nose, and saw that John was bright pink and sweating profusely. But he still retained his faculty of speech.

"I think," he said, "that I shall be ill if this little lot goes on much longer."

He was right, of course. He was.

"To women!" the host said, raising his glass.

"To women!" I mouthed. The second tumblerful wasn't as bad as the first, for the first had already numbed most of my senses. But even at that early stage I must have been quite drunk. I mistook the glass of water with which I had hoped to wash down this vitriol for a third tumbler of spirit which my kindly neighbour had already poured out for me in anticipation of the next toast. I drained it down in one. Now I was one up on the rest. Now I had the best part of a third of a bottle of almost raw alcohol inside me. I felt fine.

"A toast! A toast!" the wood-choppers cried. "Give us a toast!"

John clawed his way on to his feet and stood swaying over the table. His eyes were glassy, beads of sweat rolled down his brow, he had torn his shirt open as if to breathe more freely. He stared at the cold bowls of soup in front of him. They swilled before his eyes, he said later, like slop.

"Pig swill!" he said, half-raising his glass.

"In Russian!" the wood-choppers clamoured. "Give us a toast in Russian!"

"I give you a toast . . . " John mumbled, "I give you a toast to . . . " We all waited, swaying on our heels.

"Show business!" John said, brightly.

"Show business!"

"Show business!" the wood-choppers mimicked, dubiously.

We clinked our glasses solemnly. I threw back my head and raised my glass to my lips. But I didn't drink. I waited, simulating imbibing motions. They won't catch me with another one, I thought. But I was wrong. I caught sight of Dubrovnik watching me.

"Mr Botting! Mr. Botting!" I heard him say. "*Do dna!*"

You miserable, you ineffably unholy little man, I said to myself. You louse and son of a louse. I shall put your head through a wringer. I shall play tunes on your nackers with a drumstick. I shall grind your liver with a nutmeg grater. What I shan't do, Dubrovnik, what I shan't do! You miserable, miserable sneak. You nark. You nerd. You THING.

I drank it down.

The walls pulsed, the table spiralled down, spinning into the roaring void and surging back again; the simple wood-chopping faces swung like pendulums before me and through the trembling window I saw the trees shoot up to heaven.

I didn't feel very well.

"When I was in the Antarctic," I heard our host saying, "we washed the spirit down with snowballs . . . "

"Fermented boot-polish," John was saying. "They're going to give us fermented boot polish. And after that . . . "

"Isn't there a new law in England," someone said, "that you can't beat your wife after eleven p.m.?"

"No," John said, "midnight."

"Does that apply to the Queen?"

"Of course. Even though she's the Queen of England, Prince Philip still has the right to beat her. And he does. He does. Oh, by God, yes!"

"If I didn't beat my wife," someone else said, "I wouldn't be as fit as I am at my age."

And they all laughed and the laughter boomed between the walls like an earthquake and rolled down the table like a thunderbolt and broke my head in pieces. "Oh, mother," I heard John say, "Oh Jeeeesus," and he was laughing too and then I was laughing and we were all laughing and laughing and when I woke up it was the next day and I was lying on my bed in my clothes with a head like a broken old coconut and a stomach I didn't care to remember.

I had been very ill.

.   .   .

We flew away that afternoon. Rain was falling from a leaden sky and the airstrip, we were told, would be inoperable by morning. We escaped, taking our hangovers with us, and flew in cloud all the way to Irkutsk. Only occasionally did we catch any glimpse of the ground, of a bleak Siberia below us, cold, grey and wet. It matched our mood. By now we were tetchy invalids. We wore dark glasses and spoke in whispers. We could just manage a lightly-boiled egg.

Before we left we had signed the visitors' book. We wrote: "We admire—and even envy—the young people here. We are sorry to leave this atmosphere of peace and purpose."

Which was exact enough.

5

To the Back of Beyond

IT is a curious feature of travel in the Soviet Union—for foreigners at least—that in order to take one step forward you must often take ten steps back. Progress in any one direction is made possible only by great leaps in several other directions and if one plotted the course of one's journey on a chart it would look rather like the temperature graph of someone suffering from a violently fluctuating fever. The long, strong arm of Moscow has decreed this inconvenient and highly illogical mode of progression; a highly-developed jet transport system has made it possible. Whatever the reason for it, it remains an absurdity. If, for example, you wished to travel to the east of the country by way of Irkutsk and Khabarovsk, which are only 1,350 miles apart, you would go in this way: Moscow-Irkutsk (2,600 miles), Irkutsk-Moscow (another 2,600 miles), Moscow-Khabarovsk (3,800 miles). In other words, you would have added well over half the distance of the diameter of the earth to your journey—and well over half the contents of your purse. Thus it was that when we left Bratsk we found ourselves flying south in order to go north. We had to regain Irkutsk before we could set off to our next destination, which was the town of Yakutsk, in far north-eastern Siberia, where only a handful of westerners had been in the last decade.

Voyagers in the days before air travel did not have to endure this peculiarly Soviet form of frustration. They went, as best they could, in a straight line. On the other hand, they had to grapple with problems which the air passenger hardly dreams of, for there stretched before them 1,200 of some of the most formidable miles in the world, and a journey which to-day takes only a few hours would in those days take the best part of a whole month. The accounts these hardy travellers have left us of this route and the trials to be endured on it, make fascinating reading to-day. Browsing through them, one becomes conscious, with a little shock of surprise, that while so much has changed in recent years a great deal has not changed at all; there, one says to oneself with some relief, but for the grace of the aeroplane, go I.

The first part of the journey north used to be known as ordeal by *tarantas*. This is how a German zoologist travelling to Yakutsk in 1901 described this particular instrument of torture.

"In the early hours of the morning we packed the *tarantas*, covered it with sailcloth, and secured it as far as possible with strong ropes against slipping, and against the greater danger of theft.

"In the coach itself were mattresses, pillows and blankets. We were going to travel by night as well as through the day, but we hoped to get some sleep, as the coachman had already taken the trouble to provide a thick flooring of fresh soft straw.

"A *tarantas* holds two persons, who lie on mattresses on the floor, with pillows at their backs. There are no seats. The box seat is covered, and in rain or snow a roof can be drawn over the coach too, so that one is really quite well protected. Sleep is absolutely necessary on a long journey, and the *tarantas* would be really quite a suitable vehicle if it had not the very painful drawback of having no springs. The body of the coach rests on three thick poles which are anything but springy, but they are fastened fore and aft to axle-trees, making the carriage remarkably stable. This is essential on wretched roads.

"Three horses draw the carriage. Between the shafts there is the big, strong centre-horse, which is always a good trotter and will always keep to this gait. It is harnessed in the characteristic large hoop, which always carries three bells, for no *yamshik*, as the coachman is called, would drive without the sound of bells. The other two horses are harnessed to right and left of the centre one. They gallop in order to keep up with the trotter, who is straining on ahead in the middle.

"We hurried through Irkutsk, but nowhere in Russia are roads worse than in the towns and villages. Hole followed hole, especially in the outskirts through which we swished at a gallop. The coach jolted so that speech was impossible unless we risked losing some teeth or a bit of tongue and we bounced up and down like rubber balls. It was a fearful thought to have to get over hundreds of miles in this fashion . . .

"A few miles from the town, however, the road became rather better and our sufferings less acute. It led over a hilly countryside, and on a ridge beside a ravine a cross was standing. I had already noticed crosses like this by the road soon after leaving the town. Our driver told us that at these places travellers had been robbed and killed. It was the custom in Russia to erect a cross where anyone had been done to death; and the district round Irkutsk was very unsafe because of the number of convicts who had escaped from the mines. These crosses continually catching the eye warned us to be on our guard, and we got ready our guns. We had certainly no intention of letting ourselves be plundered by these gentlemen of the road without putting up a fight, and still less inviting was the thought that memorial crosses might have to be put up here for us."

These "gentleman of the road" —escaped convicts and vagrants known collectively as *brodnyaks*—were a very real danger to the Siberian traveller in Tsarist times. They were desperate and violent and they would kill for a crust. In some years 60,000 of them were at large and every spring, when the first cuckoo was heard, they would desert the prison camps *en masse* to join, as they put it, General Cuckoo's Army. Murder was rife then and the traveller was never far from his weapon. Not even the governors of the provinces were safe from attack by these marauding brigands, and one of them is even reported to have been robbed of his ceremonial regalia.

But it seems that the discomfort rather than the lawlessness of the roads was the traveller's main preoccupation. Their accounts all agree on one thing—that the hotels and rest-stations en route were abominable and could only be endured when nothing else was available. Substantial towns with reasonably civilised amenities were, and still are, few and far between. Most of the tiny, scattered settlements the traveller had to stop at to change horses or obtain shelter were simply miserable dumps, and to-day many of them are not very different. "There cannot be a single place in the whole wide area," wrote the German zoologist of one such station, "that so little deserves the name of town. There are a little wooden church and a few wooden houses, including those of the district officer, the priest and the storekeeper Gorochov. With these exceptions the people —comprising about fifteen Yakut families, a dozen Cossacks and about seventy-eight political exiles—live in yurts. Streets there are none. Even in the tiniest village on the Lena we saw at least footpaths, if dirty ones; but here the buildings lay far apart from each other. To reach them we usually had to wade as well as we could through swamps and puddles which, because it was summer, had a treacherous covering of green growths and so were difficult to spot. Not knowing them, we were often in danger of leaving our loose Yakut boots behind in these sticky bogholes . . . " Even those villages blessed with paths were not really so well off. "The path from the river bank led over a veritable dung heap, for the people throw their refuse, year in, year out, on to the slopes of the river bank, where it is left lying unless the water carries it away at high water. The surface of the road is of hardened dung, and it was a puzzle to us how anyone could get over this in wet weather when it softens."

It was not surprising that accommodation in such places should be of a primitive kind. To a tender but brave Englishwoman venturing across Siberia in the 1890s it was a matter of considerable concern. "And now, dear reader," she coaxed, "let me introduce you to your hotel; but have patience. The key must first of all be found, and then candles and matches. Have your pocket-handkerchief ready, if you can find it, and place it close to your nostrils the moment the door is opened. The hinges creak, and your first greeting is a gust of hot, fetid air which almost sends you back; but you remember the cold outside and the cravings of hunger, and so you go in.

"The menu is regulated entirely according to your own tastes; in fact, it consists chiefly of the viands which you have brought with you, and which do not happen to have bounced out of the sledge, or which you haven't flung to the wolves on your way. You will be badly off indeed if you cannot contrive to have a few dry biscuits and a glass of tea. There are no waiters to bother you at this hotel, and no fees of any kind; and that should relieve your mind.

"The sheepskin and rugs (none of the cleanest) are then laid in the middle of the floor. That is your bed; but don't suppose you will have sole possession of it. One glance around the walls at the number of moving specks of different sizes and families will at once dispel that illusion, whilst the probable arrival of another tardy traveller will deprive you of even the comfort of a room to yourself.

"The heat of these premises is grateful and comforting at first; but some hours before dawn you long for the intense cold outside and you register a vow that never as long as you live will you enter such a stifling hole again. But alas for human constancy! the very next night, or perhaps for many nights, you will eagerly seek the shelter of one of these warm structures and sleep soundly until awakened by a sensation of approaching suffocation.

"As for the sanitary arrangements," the good lady added, "it would be best not to mention them." From my own experience, I know exactly what she meant.

So the traveller made his painful way across steppes, through forests and over hills and ridges till he reached, some several hundred miles north of Irkutsk, the banks of the river Lena. Behind him now were the potholes, the dust and quagmire of the road, the snow melting down his neck in winter and the mosquitoes biting through his leather gloves in summer. Ahead lay the great river and a journey of three weeks and a thousand miles by barge and steamboat to Yakutsk.

Before the advent of the aeroplane the river was the only real means of communication in all the Yakutsk region, and the traveller drifted for days on end in a kind of soporific limbo between the wild and fantastic banks. Of all the rivers in Siberia, Siberians will say, none is grander or more extraordinary than the Lena, for its cliffs rise from the water like the columns of a great cathedral and the red sandstone is eroded by time and weather into sheer spires or hollowed out to form deep caves. Larches and Siberian silver-firs cling to the vertical rock-faces and beyond the banks mountain ranges run back into the vast hinterland. Occasionally there is a granite outcrop, or green porphyry and slates of different colours, and warm springs run out from the mountains into the river and spread a curious smell of hydrogen sulphide in the air around. On the first part of the journey the river is still narrow and the current swift. Sometimes boats are lost among the rocks, for even a light wind can stir the waves into tremendous breakers which will dash a small vessel against the cliffs of the bank. It is near this part, at a place called Chastye Ostrova, that the great Schoki rocks, enormous perpendicular spires 600 feet high and striped red and green, rise in gigantic rows one behind the other and glower down on the river. Their formation is so strange that it is said that a pistol shot will echo a hundred fold between them and sound like the roar of artillery. The river flows past them, moves northwards steadily to the distant ocean, doubles back on itself, loops through the forest, receives its countless tributaries and all the time constantly widens as it approaches Yakutsk until, at the town itself, it is as much as eleven miles broad and one bank is virtually out of sight of the other.

To those who had journeyed there in this way, Yakutsk, after weeks of numbing tedium and tribulations, must have seemed the height of civilisation. "There are a good many definitions of civilisation," wrote one such happy voyager. "Almost every man has his own. In this instance we decided that civilisation was the first place one came to where they sold siphons of soda-water. There is something peculiarly sophisticated about soda-water siphons when you are two thousand and more miles from a rail-head. Savages have music and art, fires, colds in the head, involved systems of ethics, and that universal sense of humour which loves to see you fall backwards out of a boat—but savages have *not* soda-water siphons. So I repeat, you reach civilisation at Yakutsk."

For the unfortunate air-traveller there are no such subtle celebrations, and the journey between Irkutsk and Yakutsk is so swift that a direct comparison of the two is inevitable. When Dubrovnik bundled us on to the five o'clock afternoon jet amidst our litter of baggage we were like two little rabbits who were bolting out of a better hole into a worse one. We were leaving civilisation, not returning to it.

The plane made two stops during the flight—one at Kirensk, 400 miles to the north; and another at a place whose name, I confess to my shame, I have not discovered to this day. Perhaps it was Olekminsk, but it doesn't really matter—it was getting dark, it was raining, and all we saw of it, wherever it was, was the inside of the airport hut. I would like to have called it something grander but all it was was a log hut full of rude wooden tables and benches and a counter where, in theory, you could obtain refreshments. In practice, however, you could obtain next to nothing. There was no bread to be had, no tea, no coffee and, worst of all, no cigarettes. All there was for sale was milk and one hard-boiled egg, which the queue of passengers at the counter bumped and bored towards with churlish enthusiasm. At one time it seemed that it would be requisitioned by one of the peasants in front of me, but when it came to my turn the egg was still there, small and solitary and unwanted, and I bought it promptly and carried it in triumph to our table. We were soon joined by the air-hostess—a blonde, plumping, sensual Russian soul who seemed to find everything funny, for never before or afterwards did I meet a Russian woman who giggled so much as a matter of habit. Perhaps she found us funny, perhaps we were the only agreeable company in that dingy shack, perhaps she had seen us carry off the egg. At any rate she came to sit with us and, since it was unlikely that we would find anything else to eat before the next day, we had to divide the egg into three equal portions. Of course, there was no cutlery and for a time we were stumped. We turned the inviolable egg over in our hands, held it up to the light, weighed it, rolled it round the table, and peeled it. The air-hostess even giggled at it but still it remained whole. Not until John, rummaging through his pockets, produced a nail file and sawed through the egg with the concentration and precision of a brain surgeon was it divided. We swallowed the portions in one gulp and sat despondent and hungry while the Russian girl giggled. Before long we were giggling too, and hysterical English laughter rang round the dull hut in the darkening Siberian spaces. For we, too, had seen the paintings on the wall.

There were several of them and they were all of the same subject; they differed only in detail. To me they seemed the acme of cruel irony, mystifying in their incongruity. Perhaps they had been chosen for the same sort of reason a sailor far out at sea will stick pin-up pictures of naked and crudely pneumatic females on the inside of his locker door—they were a reminder of what he most desired and was denied, of better times, of port, of home, a two-dimensional substitute for the figment of his dreams. Certainly the paintings on the airport walls were the very stuff of fantasy. One of them had squeezed within the edges of the canvas an unbelievable quantity of every kind of fruit— melons (whole and sliced and dripping with juice), huge bunches of grapes, great pineapples, peaches purple with ripeness, pomegranates, pears and golden, glowing oranges. Another showed much the same but had added goblets of wine and strewn bottles of champagne among the fruit; one of them, propped up in an ice-bucket, was frothing from its mouth and the bubbles sparkled across the canvas. A third painting depicted a variety of meat and game—a brace of pheasants, a duck, a goose and a roast suckingpig on a silver platter with an apple between its jaws. The hungry spectator was spared no detail; nostalgia welled up like tears; one felt terribly exiled. Pavlov himself could not have done better and, empty and deprived in this anonymous place in this land of nowhere, we stared at the pictures on the sombre walls and salivated.

We flew on. The sun sank but never quite set. A grey, wet, cloud-strewn light remained and below I could see the great Lena winding through the forest between high rocky banks, and towards the east a range of snowy mountains. The river bore a few small settlements along its banks and a few small ships upon its waters; otherwise the landscape was a desert, and always there was the grey, unleafy forest. Even so, I was sorry in some ways to be travelling so swiftly and easily and remotely. I was missing the hardships but I was also missing, I reflected, the sudden unexpected visions and delights that had made the bygone travellers' progress bearable. I was missing the sudden view at the bend in the river of the great elk stooping low to drink in the shallows and raising its enormous antlered head to sniff the dangerous evening air. I was missing the crystalline nights and the warmth and peace of the crackling wood fire among the trees; the lulling tinkle of the horse-bells, the flying squirrels, the kettle boiling by the running stream, the surprise supper of freshly-caught sturgeon, the mist on the river in the early morning, the sun rising, like the first scene in Genesis, on the silent, empty wilderness. There were no idylls when you were flying, and the details of the land were denied you.

Dawn was well under way when we landed at Yakutsk airport at half-past two. The churned-up mud of the airfield perimeter had frozen and we stumbled towards the reception building as if over a bomb-site. We pushed open the door.

The stench was extraordinary. In my diary I see I have described it as "the smell of fermenting birdseed in a crappy pet shop". Perhaps that is inexact but at least it conveys the degree of intensity, if not the precise quality, of that terrible odour. Only later did I discover that a greater part of the stench was due to a kind of wild garlic which the Yakuts devour in considerable quantities at periods of the year when no other vegetable is available. Crowd a large number of garlic-breathing Yakuts into a small confined space such as the airport waiting-room and in time the atmosphere becomes very hot and insupportably humming. But the garlic is not alone to blame, for some of the stench could be alleviated by the application of soap to the offending bodies — a Yakutsk winter makes a bath no light or frequent matter.

We endured the smell (it was as thick as gas in our lungs) sufficiently long to peer about us in the dim glow of some bare light-bulbs. There were benches crowded with slit-eyed Yakuts in all the postures of sleep; some were even stretched out on the floor or against the walls. This was the peasantry of the far north, shod in felt knee-boots, draped in baggy blue suits or long, black, quilted jackets, topped to a man with bulging caps. It needed a Goya or a Dürer to portray these strange and weather-worn faces, this huddle of unchanged mankind. The soil was in their marrows, the tall skies and the winds had furrowed their brains, and they slept or moved around us like refugees from an age we can no longer remember. I saw a wizened old woman, her skin like crinkled leather, squatting on the floor among her cloth-bundles, clutching a glass of curds in her knotty hands and staring into vacant space. I saw the ones bolt upright with their mouths fallen open in sleep; a young couple fitted together like a twin embryo as they curled on a bench; those bent forward as if in prayer; children beautiful in repose. Everywhere there was the sprawl of limbs, disarray of skirts, open hands and extended fingers, the little indignities of public sleep, the unconscious and incongruous promiscuities. It was like a battlefield, and there were even flies crawling over one man. A woman made an announcement over the loudspeaker but no one stirred—they were here for the night, waiting for the plane that would take them back to that former age at the edge of the world they knew as home.

It was evident that there was no one to meet us and we went outside to escape the stench and the disturbingly alien crowd. It was cold and I was grateful for my Canadian fur jacket, though it was no defence against the enormous and brutish mosquitoes which, even at this early hour, began to prod and poke us in their insistent way.

"If anyone *wants* to meet us," John said, his hands buried in his raincoat pockets and his head sunk disconsolately into his turned-up collar, "I would say we were as obvious as two spare ticks at a Tartar wedding."

But nobody did, and after a while we hired a car and drove at 120 kilometres an hour down deserted unmetalled streets of wooden houses to the Lena Hotel and a deep and hungry sleep at half-past three.

6

Yakutsk

YAKUTSK is the capital of Yakutia, the land of the Yakuts. Formally, at least, it is an Autonomous Soviet Socialist Republic with its own government and constitution; but in practice it is difficult to see how it differs in this respect from anywhere else in the USSR, for the octopus arms of Moscow stretch as far as here with ease and effectiveness. It is an enormous region, five times the size of France, almost as big as European Russia itself, not very much less than half the entire area of the United States. In many ways it is Siberia *in extremis*, the Siberia of anyone's preconceptions. Half of it lies inside the Arctic Circle and nearly all of it is permanently frozen, in summer as well as winter. To the north this bleak territory is bounded by the ice floes and hummocks of the Arctic Ocean; in the south are the endless tracts of empty forests and marshes. The cold pole of the world is here; rivers may freeze for as much as ten months; the sun may disappear for ten weeks at a stretch; and the darkness of midwinter may thicken still more when the black-bodied white-sheened clouds of the terrible *purga*, the Siberian snowstorm, blow across the joyless spaces and bury unwary travellers alive during a week of incessant blizzard. It is hardly surprising that less than half a million people inhabit Yakutia and that there are more reindeer than men. So empty is this inhospitable region that in 1946 the Russians were able to explode their first atomic bomb there without any elaborate safety precautions. There just wasn't anybody living for miles around.

Our first impression of Yakutsk, the capital, was that it was a one-horse town. Nothing we saw could change that impression and it hardened into a final bleak conclusion. "The town of Yakutsk," wrote a traveller at the turn of the century, "is not a pretty place, and has a dreary dead appearance. At eight o'clock the houses are shut up, and there are no amusements or recreations." The town hasn't changed very much since those days — in appearance at least. It is still largely composed of one-storey wooden huts clustered towards the river. Often they are grouped together round a courtyard, or fenced off with a plank wall; high piles of logs stand by the door for winter fuel and the pavement outside is often just a wooden plank to keep your feet clear of the mud. The residential part of the town still looks like a pioneer settlement of temporary dwellings roughly knocked together with logs and nails; the Pilgrim Fathers may well have put up something like it when they first landed in the New World. Nearer the centre of the town there are some much finer wooden houses — the bank, for example, is one of them, with fretwork balconies and tall pillars of wood like Doric columns and elaborately carved window-frames. Such traditional Russian structures represent the height of the timber architect's art and they can be very beautiful and appropriate to their setting. But they are slowly being replaced by buildings of concrete and steel which are uglier but more permanent and more prestigious. Main Street, Yakutsk, is now almost entirely lined with such buildings and it is the most forlorn street I have ever seen in any town. It is very broad like most Russian thoroughfares, and it carries very little traffic; its pavements are also broad and only moderately crowded; staring at each other across this wide, chilly gap are the vacant, unpromising, unwelcoming façades of Yakutsk's permanent buildings, like the patched and peeling cement banks of some dried-up, disused canal. Main Street, Yakutsk, is dreary indeed. There is nothing to divert you, nothing to keep you — only a few kiosks selling four-page Yakutian newspapers and strong *Kazakh* cigarettes, a cinema like a village hall, a draughty theatre and a warm baker's shop. Main Street is the town's showpiece; behind it sprawl the untidy, winter-worn shacks of an unchanged Siberia.

John and I spent our first morning in Yakutsk walking up the right-hand side of Main Street (we called it Main Street but almost certainly I think its real name was, predictably, Lenin Prospekt). Then we walked down the left-hand side. A cold, dusty wind blew down the street and we turned our collars up and tried to forget that we hadn't had any breakfast because the hotel buffet was closed. We trudged dutifully up and down for an hour and then, for want of anything else to do, turned off down a side-road and walked along a plank pavement. It was not a good time of the year to see Yakutsk—but then, I wondered, what time was? The ice on the Lena had already broken and been borne sea-wards; the river, swollen by melting snows along its course, had flooded parts of the town and now the floodwaters were receding, leaving muddy creeks and odd patches of boggy ground; every-where among the untidy huts were festering pools of water and even, at one spot, a fair-sized lake containing small fragments of opaque ice like dissolving lozenges and a miscellany of unassorted rubbish.

We walked for another hour and then turned back towards the hotel. All we had seen were the houses, the muddy streets, the Russian jeeps bumping past, drinking water being delivered to households by horse and cart (as yet there is little piped water in Yakutsk) and slant-eyed, slightly yellow, round-faced girls trotting demurely about in flat-heeled shoes, macintoshes and coloured headscarves. For all its remoteness, its out-on-a-limb-ness, Yakutsk had its full measure of that peculiarly Soviet urban virtue of dullness. It seemed there were no exotic secrets in this town, and depression seized us as we returned to the Lena Hotel.

It had not always been so in the past. Not so long ago wolves would come into town to dig up the graves, and you could see performing bears in cages and elderly yellow ladies smoking ivory pipes on the backs of bullocks. You could see the clever ivory carvers squatting in their booths and the trappers coming in from the outback with their sledges piled high with the pelts of sable, silver fox, moose, ermine, squirrel and snow wolf. There was a bishop living there then, and a cathedral, but the biggest building was the vodka factory and there were several taverns and liquor shops where beefy hunters and thirsty Yakuts and randy soldiers and all the tough-nuts and down-and-outs of Siberia's Dawson City could drink themselves stupid and fight and brawl and chase what women there might be. It was a hard territory and it made for a crude life and crude people. The mail took forty-five days to reach Yakutsk from Moscow and supplies might come in only once a year. The day the supply boat came in July the town would be *en fête* and there would be drunkenness, debauchery and even murders; afterwards, when all the goods had been sold and all the money spent, the town would lapse into a sullen silence until the next time. It was worse in the south in the neighbourhood of the gold mines of Aldan. There the gold-miners would get their year's wages in one lump sum and they would buy themselves several silk shirts, new boots, velveteen trousers and a beaver hat and proceed to blow their money on all the pleasures they had missed in their year of hard labour. Some of them would hire four men to carry them from one bar to another. Others would buy lengths of cotton cloth which they would spread on the muddy ground and dance on, bottle in hand, to the tunes of a specially hired musician. In the bars and pleasure-houses which once ringed the gold mines like the tents of a blockading army they would hire young women who had come there from the cities of Russia and Europe and they would buy for these girls of fortune fine clothes and huge hand-wrought gold rings and bracelets and satiate themselves with their much-used expensive bodies and gamble and drink till the vodka was almost running out of their ears. And then, after two or three days, the money would be gone and they would be in debt and they would have to sign on for another year working knee-deep in the icy waters of the mines. Those that were alive, that is. For many were murdered for their money and their bodies thrown in the river.

The Communist Revolution, which reached Yakutsk in the mid-1920s, changed all that—mostly for the better. Conditions ameliorated, people became more respectable, a kind of latter-day Puritanism overtook the old wild east. But even to-day Yakutsk is still a rough town; it is still the raw outback there, and occasionally one glimpses a scene that might easily have come out of the last century. The tumultuous past is not so easily disinherited.

The hotel restaurant, for example, was never a quiet place. As far as I could gather, it was the only one in town and it was always crowded from mid-morning when it opened to late evening when it closed. At peak hours it was so crowded that the padded felt and wood doors were locked and a queue of rough, impatient, angry men would wait outside it under the uneasy surveillance of a uniformed policeman. Whenever a table in the restaurant became vacant there would be a sound of a key turning and of bolts drawing back and the door would open fractionally against its strong spring. This was always the signal for a stampede, and the policeman would have to grapple forcibly with the would-be insurgents as they struggled to push through the door, pushing and arguing with each other and disregarding the policeman. But if more than the correct quota got through the door there was always the restaurant doorman to throw them out. He was a big, burly Russian and he stood no nonsense. If there was no room for the prospective client, be he Yakut or Russian, he was thrown back through the door he had entered. You needed to be a hefty wing-three-quarter to get into that restaurant at dinner time.

It was easier for us. With our dapper, Oxford Street shoes, and Marks and Spencer shirts we were immediately identifiable as strangers, and if we weren't obviously foreign to the average homespun Yakut or marooned Russian we were obviously from more genteel parts in the west of Russia, so that the status and authority of emissaries from Moscow was imputed to us. The first time we tried to enter the restaurant by jumping the queue, however, there were sullen threats from the waiting men and the policeman barred our way. It required the head waitress to come to our rescue. "Don't you know who those people are?" she scolded them, and they said no, they didn't, and when she told them the crowd withdrew reverentially to let us pass and the policeman saluted us. I thought this sort of thing was all very wrong and embarrassing—not at all what I expected of an allegedly classless society. But it was always like that. If we decided to catch a plane at very short notice we were always first on board and choosing the best seats, while some poor peasant who had booked weeks ahead was deprived of his place. It seemed that to travel in Russia comfortably and efficiently you had to be a foreigner—and a capitalist one at that. Then you got the most deferential treatment and warmest regards.

I remember the Lena Restaurant fondly as one of the most barbaric places I have ever eaten in. Not that we could complain about the service for the waitresses fluttered around us like scalded chickens; we never had to endure the usual interminable wait and whatever there was we could have. This led to some awkward situations. Only on one day was beer officially on the menu; normally if a Russian asked for it he was told there wasn't any, but we were able to order it any time we liked and when it came the waitress had taken the precaution of steaming the label off so that none of our fellow diners could recognise what it was. Invariably, though, someone spotted those anonymous bottles and would sidle up to us, a glass carefully concealed in his hand, and ask us for a helping; and after we had artfully poured it out under the table, he would drain it down in one with his back turned to the waitress, politely thank us and return to his own table and his carafe of vodka. Spirits—cognac, vodka and the terrible Siberian spirit—seemed to be the only regularly available drinks in Yakutsk and the people had an immense propensity for them; they drank abominably. Some days comatose drunks would lie asleep on the restaurant steps and the sound of vomiting in the vicinity became very familiar. It is not an offence to be drunk in the streets in Russia provided you are actually holding on to something, and one day at noon in a Yakutsk street I saw a man lying flat on his face across a pavement, dead to the world but still rigidly clinging with outstretched arms to a lamp-post;

nobody disturbed him, they just gently stepped over him if they wanted to pass, and he looked very comfortable and peaceful and more drunken than anyone I had seen in my life. On another evening, in the restaurant, I was gnawing and hacking my way through a particularly rubbery beefsteak when I saw a very old Yakut woman at a nearby table lift the edge of the tablecloth and solemnly vomit on to the floor. Then she took another long swig from her tumbler of spirit, contemplated the wall for a moment, put her hand over her mouth, lifted the edge of the table-cloth again and retched a second time under the table. No one seemed to pay any attention and her companions carried on talking as though nothing had happened. But her eyes were terribly glazed— they looked almost sightless—and when her companions poured her another drink she collapsed. That night was a peculiarly degenerate one, I don't know why. There seemed to be no special cause for celebrations, but the crowd outside the restaurant seemed bigger and more humourless than I had ever seen it before and the people inside more violently pie-eyed than usual. I saw one Yakut hit another in the teeth and then he was chucked out into the street; and I saw a Russian half-way through a window making signals to us—when there were no waitresses looking we gave him the thumbs-up and he dropped to the restaurant floor, adjusted his jacket, winked to us and sat down at an empty place. It was then that a plump, middle-aged Russian, obviously a stranger to the town, asked if he could join us. He was drunk, too, and we didn't like the way he was talking. He kept looking at us in a funny way, and smiling as if he wanted to ingratiate us, and twitching his eyebrows in what was clearly a burlesque attempt at vamping us. He talked in a maudlin way for a while and then he said, "If you wish to hear the rest of my speech we must leave this recreational centre for a quieter and—hum—more private place. You see, I love you. Both of you . . . "

We escaped to the cinema. This was a curious, dingy place with two small auditoriums on different floors where separate pro-grammes were shown simultaneously. We chose the upstairs performance and took our places on wooden chairs amongst a mixed audience of children, leathery old overcoated Yakut women and Russian workers in serge caps. The main film was preceded by a travelogue shot in Georgia and I have never seen a film of this genre stimulate so much audience-participation. Before long the camera was weaving among bunches of ripe purple grapes and examining in close-up the fine down on the skin of a succulent peach; a corporate sigh went up from the spectators when they saw these things, an exclamation of disbelief and wonderment, of longing and regret. In a town where little grew out of the frozen soil, where even potatoes seemed unobtainable (we had to eat rice instead) and the people ate wild garlic in lieu of green vegetables, the fruits of Georgia were a bitter reminder of a distant and almost unimaginable world of abundance and luxury. Whoever chose to show that film before such a deprived audience, I thought, had a macabre, sadistic streak in him. One shot, especially I remember, almost brought the house down. It began with the profile of a beautiful, raven-haired young Georgian girl; slowly, with a kind of teasing casualness, she brought a great slice of water-melon to her mouth and sank her pearly teeth and scarlet lips into the fruit's dripping flesh. The sensuality of this act was almost shocking; the juice glistened at the corners of her mouth and trickled down her chin; the citizens of wintry, benighted Yakutsk, who had watched it all in riveted silence, broke out into an uproar. It required a shot of a sturgeon fish underwater—an unprecedented view—before they ceased their agitated murmurings, but for minutes afterwards chatter on the subject of the melon buzzed like a sawfly in that murky room.

7

Yakut Man and Mammoth

THE history of Siberia, of its exploration and conquest, is as colourful and violent as that of America's wild west. From the time of Ivan the Terrible in the sixteenth century Cossack troops and rabble armies of adventurers and hunters were pushing the Tsar's dominion into the unknown fastnesses beyond the Ural Mountains. Their progress was greatly simplified by the remarkable river system of Siberia. It is possible to paddle nearly all the way across this broad land, for a network of waterways extends for 5,000 miles from west to east and portages between the different rivers are easy. This accounts for the extraordinary speed with which the penetration of Siberia was accomplished; but the zeal with which it was brought about was due to one overriding factor—furs. Siberia was a treasure-house of fur-bearing animals and their pelts were almost as valuable as gold. According to the Moscow Government's official treasury statement of 1586, Siberia provided the Tsar with 200,000 sables, 10,000 black foxes and 500,000 squirrels, beavers and ermines in that year alone. One-third of the State's income came from Siberian furs and their value was colossal—two black fox pelts, for example, could buy twenty head of cattle, five horses, scores of sheep and fowl, fifty-five acres of land with a house, and still leave half of the 110 roubles purchase price.

So great was the urge to the east that by 1628, less than fifty years after the first conquests had begun, the colonisers had got as far as the Lena river. In that year a band of ten men travelled on skis from the Yenisei to a spot not far from present-day Yakutsk and apparently were able, in spite of their small numbers, to subdue all the tribes of the region. A few years later a fort and a stockaded settlement were built at Yakutsk and the period of Russian rule began. In 1900 most of the fort was still standing; its towers and armouries of huge larch trunks were in as good a condition after 300 years as the day they were built. To-day one tower remains, a splendid survival of old brown wood amongst the concrete office blocks surrounding it.

Stories and chronicles describe that pioneer period. It was not a meek age. Life was ruthless and lives were cheap. The Yakuts themselves have their own version of the conquest of their land and the building of the first fort.

"After Yermak had conquered Siberia," the story goes, "and was drowned in the river Irtish, his lieutenant, Ivan Koltzo, said: 'Now that he is dead, why should I care for my life? I will go and fight.' Then the Cossacks went in boats along the rivers, and when they reached the end of one river they carried the boats on their shoulders to another one, and they built stockaded settlements between the two rivers. They conquered many of the natives but themselves suffered much. Sometimes they were compelled by hunger to eat their own people. At last they came to the Yakutian land. A great number of natives came to meet them, and said: 'Say, friends, what is the news?' 'I want to trade with you,' said Koltzo. 'Will you sell us as much land as a bullock's hide will enclose?' It was done. The Yakuts were stupid savages then and they are stupid savages now. Koltzo deceived them. He cut the bull's hide into thin strips and with them enclosed a large area of land, built a tower on it and said: 'Now I am going to fight you.'

"And they fought. The Yakuts had their great warrior chief Dygyn. They say his shoulders were three yards round. The cossacks stayed in their tower and shot with their guns, and the Yakuts sent their arrows back to the Cossacks. Dygyn was thinking. The Cossacks had no food, and they came out of their tower to get some. Now they had a very bad time. Dygyn was a very brave warrior. He killed a great many Cossacks but nobody could kill him. Then Ivan Koltzo played a trick. The Cossacks

Yakut hunter in the tundra.

John Bayliss and Douglas Botting pose with helicopter crew and reindeer herdsmen in the tundra near Kolyma.

A reindeer herdsman of the far north with the necessities of his life—gun, dog and reindeer.

Afanasi the Chukchi.

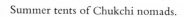

Summer tents of Chukchi nomads.

Reindeer herd in full gallop.

The ice of the Kolyma river cracking up in June.

The limitless tundra of north-east Siberia.

Up-country Armenians.

The heavy horse-hair veil of Uzbek women is a rarity now.

hung out a heavy block from the tower, and under it they placed all kinds of dolls and ribbons. Then Koltzo sent a message to the Yakuts: 'Let us have peace. Come to us as friends.' The foolish Yakuts believed him and went to the tower. While they were looking at the dolls and ribbons Koltzo ordered the Cossacks to cut the cords holding up the block. It fell down and crushed them all and they all died. Koltzo tore out Dygyn's eye, put it in spirit and sent it to the Tsar. That was an eye indeed; it weighed thirty pounds. But the Tsar said: 'Why did you not bring me this giant alive?'

"And from that time the whole of the region was the Tsar's. The Yakuts ran away to the forest, to the marshes, to the mountains, and the Government could hardly find them afterwards."

Which was just as well, for the Government was brutal and tyrannical in the extreme. When, after years of extortion and torture, the Yakuts finally rebelled against their Russian over-lords they were mercilessly subdued and those who were taken prisoner had their noses and ears cut off and their eyes put out, or were buried alive in the ground up to their eyes. According to a Yakut manuscript chronicle, *The Officials of Yakutsk and Their Doings*, one governor, Barmishov by name, never sat down at table without having sentenced someone to death—often for the most trivial offence. His victims were variously quartered, impaled, boiled alive in a cauldron or, on days when he was in a good humour, simply strung up. His successor quelled a final attempt at rebellion by flaying the leader alive. The unfortunate victim's newborn child was wrapped in the skin and his wife was stretched on the rack.

That terrible death marked, more or less, the end of Yakut resistance. They settled back to accept the remote, capricious, tenuous dominance of a Tsar they had never seen and would never see, and took up again the simple, starkly rural life which they had always lived and would live until the present century and the Revolution which changed everybody's lot. Yakutsk itself grew into a vaguely European town that attracted, with a hollow promise of riches in untapped virgin territories, the foot-loose adventurers, traders, explorers and fur-trappers of succeeding centuries. Expeditions of discovery set out from there, nosing up the Lena and along the unknown Arctic shore; some came to grief, others found new lands, new passages and routes to the Pacific; one of them landed and laid claim to Alaska, so that for a time a part of the USA lay under the rule of the Tsars. The Yakuts stayed at home and festered contentedly in their native bogs.

Not that they were by any means as backward as most of the other tribes of this bleak region. Instead of diminishing in numbers or dying out altogether as a result of the ravages of smallpox and syphilis—new diseases to which many aboriginals of northern Siberia succumbed after contact with the Russian colonists—the Yakuts multiplied. From merely occupying a limited area around Yakutsk they spread out into the surrounding territory and grew in numbers until today they are the main population of the entire Lena basin and totalled more than a quarter-million persons at the last census. The hardiness that enabled them to survive their forced migration from their original homeland in the neighbourhood of Lake Baikal and to adapt themselves to life in the far severer conditions of the north also enabled them to survive the Cossacks and Russian fur-traders and later the exiled criminals who were sent there in ever-increasing numbers. They successfully changed the basis of their economy from horse-breeding (which they still practise) to cattle-rearing, in spite of the fact that the cattle had to be kept indoors and fed for the greater part of the year. Although subservient to the government imposed on them, they retained their native ingenuity, their national identity, their crafts, customs and language. In some of the remoter spots the Russian community gradually forgot their own language and adopted that of their Yakut neighbours, a guttural tongue related to the Turkish family; mixed marriages were frequent (at the turn of the century a Russian could still buy a Yakut girl for a block of tea and a cup of vodka) and it was not unusual for Russians to regress so far in this harsh environment that their way of life became indistinguishable from that of the native Yakuts. After their initial, savage defeat, the Yakuts slowly won back the ascendancy; in a way, it was the conquerors who were eventually conquered. The Yakut culture prevailed.

There is no doubt that in its prime, before the massive acculturation processes that followed the Soviet Revolution, the Yakut culture was a relatively advanced and distinctive one. When they were driven from the shores of Lake Baikal by the fierce Buryat nomads, they brought with them to the ice deserts of Yakutia such words as "iron", "agriculture", "to read", "to write", "letter", and even "learned". They became expert craftsman in ivory carving, silverwork and the art of the blacksmith; alone among the native peoples of that territory they knew the techniques of pottery, and they made beautiful and functional articles of leather and furs and even of bark. They were bright people, skilled with their hands, resourceful, resilient and quick to learn new crafts and ideas from the Russians. They still are.

A fortunate few among the Yakuts, some of a rich minority, were able to enjoy some form of schooling, bad as it was; one or two even got as far as University, where they were keen and intelligent students. But for the vast majority life until thirty or forty years ago was what it had always been; even to-day aspects of this age-old existence still survive.

The centre of Yakut life, the permanent home round which family and communal life revolved, was the yurt; though the Yakuts are fast moving into more spacious wooden houses, the yurt still exists in the remoter parts of the country. The traditional yurt is a simple affair using what materials happen to be to hand; it is solidly built, as warm as an oven and as smelly as a pig sty. Four thick poles are driven into the ground at the corners and they are joined by a framework of beams. Planks are laid across the beams to form the roof and the whole structure is plastered ten inches thick with a mixture of mud and dung. When this has dried the yurt is covered with earth to make it warmer, and the four little window spaces are filled with blocks of ice, or with glass if the owner can afford it. The resulting edifice looks like a mole-heap, and the low, narrow entrance — always facing east—adds to the likeness. Inside, the focus of life is the fireplace and the fire which is never allowed to go out; the hearth is of stone and the chimney of backward-sloping logs; round the fire are ranged benches covered in deer-skins. To a stranger the winter yurt has never been a great source of comfort; often the chimney is stopped up to keep out cold draughts, and the family's livestock roams about freely, with a result that the stench and the acrid smoke are almost insufferable, even in summer when the windows are covered only in thick plaits of horse-hair to keep out the flies and mosquitoes. But to the Yakut the yurt is the promise of warmth and ease out of the long, black, terrifying winter.

The yurt-dweller often has an infallible sign of the ending of winter, for then the ice in the chinks between the logs will melt and soak him to the skin. This happy event ushers in the brief northern season of abundance, when the pastoralists will move their herds of cattle, horses or reindeer to the summer grazing grounds beside the banks of the innumerable lakes of the region, where there is plenty of lush grass for pasturage and hay-making, and it is warm enough to live in simple tents of reindeer hide. This is the season of festivities, of weddings and customary celebrations; on such occasions, especially at the great koumiss festivals at the beginning and end of summer, the fats of the land are gathered together to form a banquet whose list of delicacies would make even a European gourmet tremble in anticipation. Pride of place is given to the Yakut national drink, koumiss, the symbol of plenty, which is made from fermented mares' milk. This is cooled in ice and served out, traditionally, in beakers of larchwood; it is slightly effervescent, rather sour, not very alcoholic but wonderfully refreshing. Russian vodka adds some body to the Yakuts' copious consumption of liquor and after a long day of hard drinking many of them are in a very intoxicated condition. Meanwhile the food is prepared. Oxen, reindeer and—most favoured of all—young foals are roasted on open-air spits. The national dish called *salamat*, a preparation of meal and melted butter, bubbles in iron cauldrons. All the marvellous bounty of the short summer is made ready—salmon, turbot, carp, tench, grayling and pike from the teeming, newly-flowing rivers; ptarmigan, woodcock, wild duck, goose and swan; great bowls of sweet, whipped cream, mixed with honey, bilberries and (strange choice) salmon roe; special delicacies like the udders of cows, mares and reindeer, and the lips and tongues of elk and reindeer grilled in butter. "May your mouth always be rinsed with melted butter," one Yakut will say to his neighbour as he totally consumes a pot of *salamat* twenty inches deep. "May your teeth be stuck in marrow-bones for ever," comes the reply. The Yakut's capacity for eating and drinking on these rare festive occasions is incredible; as if to make up for the meagreness of all the other days of the year, he will cram enough into his belly to last him for weeks; hiccoughing, he will fall asleep from satiety.

A festival such as this occurred when I was staying in Yakutsk. All the Yakuts of the neighbourhood gathered one day on the meadows beside the river; they drank, they ate, they danced in circles, they wrestled, they sang in nasal monotones, they played blind man's buff and the boys and girls made eyes at each other; it all seemed very traditional except for one fact—they all wore European clothes of a very cheap and ill-fitting sort, and the conglomeration of straw hats and baggy blue country suits, cheap ready-made frocks and flat-heeled shoes, gave to the otherwise gay crowd a ramshackle, tawdry air. Like a repertory company in straitened circumstances, it seemed that they were performing a pageant spectacle without the necessary props and costumes; *Chu Chin Chow* in blue-jeans and sweat-shirts; an uneasy collision of cultures. Gone were the treasured fineries from the family chest, the heirloom caftans of scarlet cloth, trimmed with beaver, lined with squirrel, extravagantly brocaded in gold; I saw no hunting knives inlaid in silver hanging from broad silver belts, no girls with rings on every finger and long earrings of silver filigree; no high beaver hats tufted in gold, no shirts of Chinese silk. Where had they gone, these customary

adornments of yesteryear? To the Folk Department of the State
Museum, along with so much else of the old ways?

Certainly a great deal had gone, and, though there may still be
an outward show of the old native culture, there is little left of the
fundamental beliefs and moral practices of a generation or two ago.
There was a time when a Yakut god lurked in every stone and
stick of furniture and tree and animal; when a god dwelt in each
of the four corners of the sky, and the Lord of All Evils, with a
mouth in the back of his head and eyes in his temples, stalked the
earth. All the many divers gods of this complex pagan pantheon
were vaguely ruled by the Drowsy Spirit of the Eight-Sided
Universe, but not even the wisest elder of the tribe could accurately
describe this exalted, sleepy deity; instead they all suffered
under Ulu-Tayon, the most terrible god of all, whom they saw
everywhere with their own eyes in the incarnate shape of a bear.
All the gods but one plagued the pagan Yakut; all disasters,
hardships, illness and death were retribution for some wrong-
doing, some failure in adequate propitiation. Obviously life
under such circumstances would have been intolerable, an endless
round of terrors, had there not been some form of defence against
the malevolent snipings of the deities. That defence was the
shaman, the long-haired, wild-eyed medicine man and priest of
the tribe, who alone had power to commune with the supernatural
world, escort the souls of the dead to their posthumous home and
intercede against the gods on behalf of man. He was at once the
mystic seer, the poet, the sage and the guardian of the tribe;
he was the repository of its lore and the healer of its sick.

Shamanism was for long a phenomenon characteristic of the
natives of Siberia, although it was not confined entirely to them.
Some authorities have explained its prevalence there on the
grounds that it was simply a ritualised form of Arctic hysteria,
a neurotic condition peculiar to Siberia. Arctic hysteria is
basically a mimicry mania. Whatever the victim hears or sees
he repeats. He may repeat words he does not even understand or
he may imitate the noises of animals. The Yakuts call such
people—they are mostly women—*emiriatchka*; sometimes, for their

own amusement, young people will stand on their heads in the presence of an *emiriatchka*, or turn cartwheels, and she will compulsively imitate them until she drops from exhaustion. Occasionally this hysteria is infectious; at village dances the rhythm may become too strong and overpowering and even the aged will be caught up in the mass emotion and swirl to the music till they collapse. Probably the unbroken monotony of life in the far north is the underlying cause of this compulsive neurosis, for it occurs not only among the Yakuts themselves, but among Russians and others who have to endure prolonged periods of inactivity in the mournful wilderness of northern Siberia. Prisoners-of-war were especially susceptible, and I have read of one German ex-officer in Siberia who roamed all over the prison-camp, unable to stop anywhere, repeating in a loud and booming voice the word "dismal" in a dozen different languages; and another who believed he was a descendant of Arpad, the conqueror of Hungary, by way of Tuhutum, the legendary sorcerer, and cheerfully and constantly repeated the motto, "Life is death and death is life," at every hour of the day until he was carted off to the psychopathic ward.

In many ways the shaman's behaviour was similar to this curious madness. His abstraction from the real world, his manic dreams and hallucinations, his ecstatic trances—all could be interpreted as symptoms of Arctic hysteria. But they could also be interpreted in terms of the razor-edge no-man's-land between inspiration and lunacy which has marked the career of many prophets and mystics in many religions. Certainly the neophyte who aspired to be shaman had first to recognise his pathological condition, interpret the crisis as a religious experience and attempt to cure himself before he could be chosen; only if he succeeded in passing this trial could he be initiated into the mysteries, for by his symbolic death and resurrection he acquired a new mode of being, he could see the spirits of the universe and himself leave his body like a spirit and soar in ecstasy through the cosmic regions. By the techniques of ecstasy he could become transported and communicate with the gods, and it was in this condition that he was best known to outsiders. Since sickness was thought to be caused by a devil entering the body of the victim, it followed that only the shaman, who had special knowledge of diseases and their cures, could deal with it. Beating his flat drum in an insistent, hypnotic, accelerating rhythm; gyrating in the firelight of the hut, his sacred robes swirling, his lips flecked with foam; uttering strange, incomprehensible words, he attained at last to a trance-like exaltation and his spirit "went out on the sound of the drum to the western heavens, to the top of the mountain where there is no day but continual night, where there is always mist and the moon is but a thin crescent". It was then that he communed with the spirits, made his oracular, inspired pronouncement and afterwards slumped to the floor.

The shamans seem to have had little say in the morality of the tribe and the Yakuts were for long notoriously loose-livers. Incest was not uncommon. Infidelity was frequent, but sexual jealousy almost unheard of. "A woman is not a roll for one man's meal," the men would say. "I am wedded but not sold," is how a woman would justify her promiscuity. The results of what we would call illicit love could be justified: "Any mare may bear a colt," the Yakuts would say, "any egg may go bad, any girl may have a child." The expression is characteristic; for all their muddy morality the Yakuts spoke in almost poetic imagery. Like many primitive people with limited concepts and limited vocabulary, they thought in pictures and spoke in parables. Mostly incapable of analytic or abstract thought, their imagination flowered with an almost lyric beauty round the familiar objects of their life. Thus winter was called "the season when water dies". Fire was known lovingly as "the grand lady who opens out her warm wraps of striped sable", while the fire-god was "the talkative little old man in bright red fox-skins". Illiterate, superstitious, immoral, primitive — nevertheless, the Yakut could strike sparks from words where the civilized man was often inarticulate and dumb.

The shamans have all gone now and the tombs of the most revered of them have rotted away after years of neglect; a new order has taken their place, a new way of thinking, a new way of living. To-day the Yakuts are moving out of their yurts into permanent houses of wood or stone; nomadism is being slowly abolished; in the warmer alluvial soil of the south agriculture has been developed, while the fishing, hunting and livestock-breeding of the north is now organised into profitable collectives. The Soviet Government has gone to considerable lengths to foster the national Yakut culture, at least where this is compatible with Socialism and contemporary values; children are taught in the schools in their own language, and theatres, publishing houses and newspapers promote a distinctively Yakutian talent in literature and music. Theoretically, the Yakut can get the best of both worlds.

To what extent the Soviets have totally eliminated the old Yakut life is difficult to determine. Undoubtedly in the towns there is little evidence that the native Yakut lives in any essentially different way from most Soviet citizens everywhere; he dresses like a Russian, eats like a Russian, lives in a proper house like a Russian, goes to school for a regular and thoroughly Russian education, accepts the Socialist ideology of the Russian, has no formal religion, considers himself a Soviet citizen first and a Yakut second and is equally happy speaking either Russian or Yakutian. But I am sure that there must still be a section of the Yakut population—perhaps just the older members of remote communities in the outback—who have been only superficially absorbed into the Soviet scheme of things, who merely pay lip service to the new ideals while in reality they adhere to the old ways and the old modes of thought and behaviour. But they must be few by now—and doomed, too; the relentless cycle of human change has overtaken them and no doubt they are derided by their younger kinsmen who have been to college and University and been imbued with the peculiarly Soviet materialistic and scientific version of modern progress.

There is no point in regretting the passing of a strange and exotic way of life. It had, in the end, little to offer the average poor man. One may have very profound doubts about the prospect of adopting Communism in one's own country or other highly-developed countries; but in such underprivileged territories as Yakutia, where famine was the overriding concern of everyone and an entire family might have to banquet on a fieldmouse, brew tea from bilberries and smoke suede leather, where diseases rampaged unchecked and the only doctors were wild shamans with maniac eyes and a futile, ecstatic repertoire of mumbo-jumbo, the Soviets have brought far more good than ill. No longer is the Yakut brutalised and his daughter sold into a brothel; no longer is he a second-class citizen, cheated by every trader in town. Today he enjoys the same rights and opportunities as any Russian; he can equally avail himself of the growing number of schools, institutes, hospitals and other essential facilities; he is no longer deprived of the bare necessities of life or of a modest share in the new Utopia; his expectation of life has probably doubled. I never saw in Yakutia (nor anywhere else in the Soviet Union) any child who was hungry, dirty or diseased, but I have seen plenty in other countries where the basic conditions for human existence were far less unfavourable. More than that, a Yakutian child, who less than forty years ago was totally denied everything that we would reasonably expect a child should have, can now look forward to a future where his every talent will be nurtured to the full. The boy who yesterday would have grown into a stunted, rickety, illiterate man, looking after cows and praying to the sun, can to-day become a distinguished scientist, artist or administrator in one of the two most powerful nations the world has ever known.

During our stay in Yakutsk we met some of the new élite of Yakutia. There was Yevdokya Stepanova, a beautiful young ballerina, who danced specially for us in the little Musical and Dramatic Theatre. In a traditional national costume, modified to suit the conventions of classical European ballet, she did the *Dance with a Tcharon* (the larchwood koumiss vessel) and an excerpt from a modern Yakut ballet in classical style called *Flower of the Field*. She had trained at the Leningrad Ballet School, had been working in Yakutsk for three years now and at the age of twenty-six had the privilege of her own flat in a two-storeyed wooden house in the suburbs. We drove her home afterwards and she was very sweet and intelligent and demure.

Then there was Niki, the local TV and news cameraman, a nervously energetic and intense young man of twenty-five or so, who had been trained for several years at the Moscow Film School. He helped us out with lighting equipment when we needed it, and even took some photos for us when we couldn't take them ourselves. He was fascinated by our German and Japanese cameras, which were better than his Russian ones, and he chewed the cardboard tubes of his *papirosi* cigarettes as a Chicago hood would chew cigar-butts, rolling them from side to side in his mouth long after they had gone out. We presented him with a pair of simple nail-clippers when we left; he had never seen such things before and when we gave them to him we became his friends for life. Niki was typical of the modern Soviet Asian; he seemed to have no consciousness of race or of the fact that he came from a minority and alien population; his Mongolian slit-eyes and squashy oriental nose were meaningless distinctions to him, for he regarded himself as a Soviet citizen first and a Yakut only second; Russian, Yakut, same thing—almost.

Some of the time we went around with Niki, who had little political consciousness and was pleasant and undemanding company but most of the time we were accompanied by Yuri, the bespectacled, besuited local *Pravda* assistant editor and *Tass* correspondent, whom we always referred to as Charlie Chan, or, if we were particularly peeved, as Charlie Chan the Two-Time Yak Man. Charlie Chan was full of political consciousness. This took the form of very arbitrary and petty decrees as to what we could and could not photograph. Unlike Niki, who did not regard us as potential agents of anti-Soviet propaganda and was, therefore, unembarrassed at some of the things we saw in Yakutsk, Charlie Chan viewed us with considerable distrust and prohibited us from photographing forest-fires, cars stuck in mud, peasants, horses and carts, wooden houses, nomads' tents and cowsheds—in short, most of the things we considered gave Yakutsk its distinctive character. We could not persuade him that our intention was not to do his country down, but we often felt like it, just for spite. He was also a walking Sphinx, inscrutable, unpredictable and oriental to a degree. Take his sense of humour. Say something like, "I wouldn't mind a glass of tea," or "I think to-morrow it will rain," and he would giggle like a maniac—a strange, very high-pitched, female shriek. But make some harmless little joke and he would glower at us as if we had just called Lenin a bald-headed loon.

It was at the Institute for Cosmo-Physical Research, housed in a small, disused church, that we were introduced to one of Yakutia's most brilliant new products—a young Yakut scientist who had recently been made an Academician of the Soviet Academy of Sciences, one of the highest scientific honours in the land. He was one of four research scientists, including the Director of the Institute, Dr Schaeffer, who solemnly lectured us for an hour, in Russian, on the nature of the work they were doing. Afterwards we went on to the Institut Merzlotavedeniye, the Permafrost Research Institute, where another Yakut scientist took us in charge and led us from a well-appointed, carpeted office into a shed covering a shaft sunk into the bowels of the Yakutian earth. At the top of the shaft we put on fur hats and quilted kapok jackets; then descended a wooden stairway into a region of never-ending ice. At only a few feet below the earth's surface the frosty walls of the shaft glittered in the electric light and the temperature fell suddenly to below freezing; at the bottom of the shaft, fifty feet below the ground, it was very cold indeed.

Our Yakut guide in this ice-cave laboratory insisted on speaking English. He had never spoken it with Englishmen before and he was totally unidiomatic; he had learnt the language in order to read English and American scientific publications, with the result that his conversation was curiously formal and larded with jargon and words that exist only in print.

"You have no permafrost in your nation, I suppose," he said as we walked down a tunnel cut into the frozen sub-soil. "In Siberia the phenomenon it will be agreed is the severer in the world entirely. To a depth it attains not in excess of 700 metres. You would say in the nature of 2,000 feets approximate, I suppose. You understand me? You understand my disquisition?"

The tunnel led to a low cave hollowed out of the frozen, sandy soil. No props were necessary, for the ice kept the ground as rigid and hard as concrete; at Tiksi, on the mouth of the Lena, there were coal mines with sixty-five foot high vaults requiring no supports whatsoever, so our scientist-guide told us; but should the ground ever warm up, the ice that bound the sand, gravel and rocks together would melt and all would subside into a muddy morass.

"*Merzlota*—permafrost—extends to include one-quarter of the earth's surface," the Yakut continued. "In the Soviet Union one-half is frozen permanent. In Yakutia the entire region is subject to it. It attains a depth here of in excess of 200 metres. It is severe, I suppose."

The walls of the cave, where the electric lamps had melted the immediate area of ice, were covered in dry, white, powdery frost; otherwise they might have been carved out of granite, though one could easily rub off the sand with one's fingers. Neatly arranged on shelves against the ice wall were permafrost exhibits—cylinder-shaped samples of the Yakutian soil in which the sand and gravel, loosely cemented by ice, looked like pork brawn in a gelatine casing.

"Permafrost is as impervious to water as clay," the guide went on. "And to pressures it is as resistant as bedrock. It causes many problems. I may give you examples, I suppose. For example, it renders difficult the supply of drinking water for domestic purposes, because water-pipes would freeze and burst immediately. Same with sewers. And solifluction and the instability of the ground cause the destruction of roads and damage to bridges and make mining difficult. Should there be an occasion for an explorer to succumb to the severity of the climate he would require to be buried above the ground, or with the assistance of dynamite. In the case of buildings I may add they are liable to subsiding in instances when their warmth causes the permafrost beneath them to melt. I have seen a house full to the roof with ice and icicles depending—suspending, yes?—

from the windows. Permafrost is difficult to the civil engineer. That is why we study it at this Institute. Our data will be used for the practical realities of building and canalisation in such temperatures."

Six feet below the Yakutsk earth the temperature was a constant —4°C. Thus the cave laboratory was considerably warmer in winter than the surface, where the temperature might fall as low as —50°C; while during the few hot weeks of summer, when the permafrost would melt to a depth of between eighteen inches and several feet, it was a refreshingly cool refuge from the heat and mosquitoes. But permafrost is not as permanent as it seems. It is now a reasonably established fact that the Arctic has been growing warmer during this century: glaciers have been retreating; sea pack-ice is thinner; birds, animals and fish have been venturing further north than they used to. This steady amelioration of the northern climate has had its effect on the permafrost regions; permafrost has been retreating northwards at the astonishing rate of one kilometre a year. If it disappeared altogether, I wonder, would Yakutia sink without trace into a bottomless quagmire?

With the help of research institutes like the one at Yakutsk Soviet scientists and engineers have made considerable headway against the peculiar problems of permafrost. To-day in Yakutsk they are putting up large four- and five-storey buildings of brick and concrete by the simple, but costly, expedient of boring deep into the frozen ground with hot jets of steam and then sinking concrete piles into the holes; these piles serve as stilts on which the foundations of the buildings are laid, thus ensuring a deep layer of insulating air between the warm floors and the ground. These techniques have proved so practicable that plans for twelve-storey buildings are now on the drawing-board, though they will cost three times as much as conventional buildings of the same dimensions. Main water pipes can also be laid below ground so long as the water circulates; if it is pre-heated at its delivery point it will still be above freezing on its return, provided it flows swiftly enough. Sewer pipes can be laid along-side the warm water-pipes, or laid above ground in heavily

revenue of the natives of Yakutia. Some mammoth tusks have been found measuring up to twelve feet nine inches in length and weighing 165 lb., and they found a good price in the ivory markets of the civilised world.

Of the mammoth remains discovered in Siberia since the eighteenth century some have been found in a remarkable state of preservation, with tusks, hair, wool, skin, flesh, blood and stomach contents preserved intact by the ice tomb in which they were originally buried. Indeed, in the few days before decay sets in as a result of exposure to the warm surface air, the meat of the mammoth is perfectly edible and can be fed to dogs and even to humans if they are sufficiently hungry not to be squeamish. One Soviet geological expedition, marooned and starving in northern Siberia, is supposed to have survived by dining for some weeks on the abundant flesh of a mammoth discovered by chance during their wanderings. This story may be apocryphal, but it is perfectly feasible, for most of the mammoth carcases that have so far been discovered whole died not as a result of old age or disease but from suffocation or exposure after accidentally sinking into bogs or crevasses which then froze round them. Such carcases thus resembled freshly butchered meat kept overlong in a deep-freeze.

Claims have occasionally been made that mammoths can still be seen alive in remoter corners of Siberia. For that matter claims have also been made that dinosaurs inhabit a lake called Labankur, high up in the mountains. Once, so Siberians will tell you, a reindeer was pushed into this lake and when it reached the middle a monster rose from the water, seized the reindeer and disappeared with it into the icy depths. Siberia is the sort of country that breeds such stories. It can safely be said that no dinosaurs — they were warm weather creatures — can possibly be alive in Siberia to-day; and, though I am sure no mammoths exist either, it is less easy to see why they failed to survive, for they were well adapted to life in conditions that are little different now from what they were in the mammoth's heyday. From examinations of his preserved remains, it is clear that the mammoth was well-protected against the extreme cold by his long, coarse, black hair and thick red-brown under wool. From food remains found in his teeth and stomach, it is equally clear that the mammoth was able to find sustenance from the same vegetation as grows to-day in the areas where he ultimately met his doom — on grass, wild flowers, leaves, and the cones of firs and pines along the river banks. The conditions of north-east Siberia were not always ideal even for an Ice-Age creature like the mammoth; food was never abundant in winter and water could be as scarce on the tundra in summer as it is in the Sahara. But the glutton, the polar bear, the wolf, the elk and the reindeer — the mammoth's contemporaries — have survived to the present time in spite of such conditions. Why didn't the mammoth?

The answer, probably, is man. Man hunted the mammoth in Europe as he hunts the elephant in Africa now. The mammoth was a big, slow-moving, unmistakeable target for the arrows and spears of primitive hunters, and he was easy to trap. To the early palaeolithic inhabitants of north-east Siberia the mammoth was probably the biggest windfall of meat they could hope for in a land where sources of food could be few and far between. So they hunted the mammoth, ate its flesh, utilised its fur, and turned its tusks — as they still do to-day — into arrowheads, implements and ornaments. The last of the hairy elephants, who had sought their ultimate refuge in the farthest corners of Yakutia, were pursued even in those inhospitable regions; unlike other animals who could escape the terrible winters by moving south, the mammoth was pinned down by fear of man; the last desperate act of the species seems to have been a migration even further north, across the sea-ice to the New Siberian Islands, where their remains have been found in even greater abundance than in any other region.

And so he went out, along with the woolly rhinoceros, the bison, the saiga antelope, the wild horse and the sabre-toothed tiger, who were all once denizens of ancient Siberia; and, though carcases of his kind must still remain, perfect in all their details and proportions, frozen and uncorrupted in the permafrost of Yakutia, they are dead, and the species is quite, quite extinct.

There is something very terrible about the end of a living species, no matter how antediluvian, useless or inimical to man; and while there is no point in becoming sentimental about a huge and rather splendid animal that died out 15,000 years ago, one is aware that many other species have followed it to extinction and that the process is continuing in the present time. In Siberia, for example, the animal population has been considerably reduced as a result of over-hunting and the systematic encroachment of man. This region still has a remarkable variety of wild life (over 200 species of birds and 150 species of mammals) but the revenue from furs is less than it was in the past. Some animals, such as the beaver, have been almost totally exterminated; the few that remain have been collected together and placed in reserves. Others, like the wolves, have not long to go; to-day they are being methodically wiped out by hunters using helicopters and machine-guns. Certain of the valuable fur-bearing species that fare well in captivity are being farmed, and though hunting and trapping are still important occupations in territories like Yakutia, the fur farm seems to offer the best prospects for the survival of these species and the boosting of the industry that is based on them. One day I visited a State fur farm at Pokrovsk, some miles to the south of Yakutsk. It was large, efficient and depressing. In row after row of bare cages lived 300 silver foxes and 300 mink; they were fed, they bred, and they were killed when their winter coats had reached their prime; in any one year the farm would produce up to 2,000 skins, each of which might fetch thirty roubles in the annual Leningrad sale.

To end up as a pelt at an auction is, paradoxically, one way of surviving; to end up on a ranch or in a zoo is another. If only they could have hung on just a little longer it is possible that we might still be able to stare in wonder at the great old mammoth in his concrete paddock in the Moscow Zoological Gardens, and feed buns to the woolly rhinoceros. But it was not to be. Evolution, and man, did them in.

8

The Amazing Miss Marsden

I WAS passing a few moments in a second-hand book-shop some weeks ago, squinting at the old, dusty, dull volumes on the cluttered shelves, when I saw a title that gently nudged my memory and led me far away from that dim shop. The gold lettering on the spine of the book had faded badly in the seventy years since it had been printed, and only the last part of the title was clearly decipherable: *To Outcast Siberian Lepers*. But the name of the author stood out boldly and aroused my curiosity; I had heard that name before, and it was a Russian who had pronounced it.

"Kate Marsden?" he had said. "You've never heard of Kate Marsden? But she was an Englishwoman. You must—surely you must—have heard the name?" and he looked from one to the other of us, quizzing our blank faces for some sign of cognisance. The old clock ticked loudly on the wall of the Curator's office in the Yakutsk Museum. Marsden? Kate Marsden? We shook our heads.

The Curator sighed. "I thought you might have known of her. I've been writing a book about her, you see, the story of her life. I sent an article about her to the London *Times* once, but I never received an acknowledgement. Perhaps she's better known in Siberia than in England."

"What did she do?" John asked.

"She was a most remarkable woman. Truly amazing in the things she did. She was—I am sure this is true—the *only* foreigner ever to come to the aid of the poor people of Yakutia. The only one. And she did it all by herself." He stared through the grimy window at the muddy courtyard outside and the palisade of larch stakes that enclosed it. Could it be true that these Englishmen, Mister Bayliss and Mister Botting, had never heard of the subject of his book, the subject of his months and years of devoted research? If she had been Russian she would not have gone so unhonoured.

"She came here, to Yakutsk, of her own accord. It was a time when no one in their senses would venture into Siberia, still less into Yakutia. For a maiden lady, a foreigner, to come here unaccompanied and travel in the wildest and most terrible regions of all was an unheard-of thing, But Kate Marsden came. She suffered a great deal. Perhaps her experiences drove her out of her wits a little. But she survived them, and she succeeded in the work she had set herself. The people of this country seventy years ago owed a great deal to her. A great deal. It was thanks to her that the very first leper hospital was set up in Yakutsk. If it hadn't been for her no one would have cared about the thousands of poor lepers who lived and died here in utter misery and destitution. That was in Tsarist times. of course," he added hastily. "Things are different now."

"She sounds a formidable woman," John said.

"Yes. When you return to England you must find out about her. And you might ask the editor of the *Times* what he did with my article."

I had forgotten this incident until I saw Kate Marsden's name on that tattered volume in the bookshop. I pulled it down from the shelf.

On Sledge and Horseback to Outcast Siberian Lepers is a curious work, a period-piece *par excellence*. The advertisements at the back for example, are a sheer delight—a perfect decoction of the age in which they were conceived. Here you are invited to contemplate the purchase of a pair of Perfect Hygiene Shoes (calf leather, 10s. 6d.) "of sufficient elegance to commend themselves to the eye": or sample HRH Prince Albert's Cachoux, "Dainty Morsels in the form of tiny Silver Bullets, which dissolve in the mouth, and surrender to the breath their hidden fragrance." You are asked, through the intermediary of The Rescue Society, to spare a thought (and a donation) "for reckless girls on the brink of ruin . . . country lasses, penniless in the world's richest city, in danger of a fate worse than death"; while the agents for Count Mattei's Marvellous Medicines (for leprosy, malaria, dysentery, piles, varicose veins, tumours, colds, acidity, sea-sickness, bronchitis and skin diseases) insist, with commendable honesty, that "the magical and marvellous operation of these Remedies is a perpetual surprise". Stanley, the African explorer; the doctor to Emin Pasha's Relief Expedition; Nansen, the Arctic traveller ("I have now used Bovril in various ways, and I like it very much") have all added their historic comments to the various goods advertised. Even Miss Marsden was solicited, and she had to confess that she owed her life to the woollies which Dr Jaeger's Sanitary Woollen System Company Ltd. had persuaded her to wear on her dangerous mission to the interior of Siberia.

Glued to the fly-leaf of Kate Marsden's book is the facsimile of a letter from Queen Victoria's private secretary, despatched to her from Balmoral Castle ("The Queen has taken a deep interest in the work undertaken by Miss Marsden amongst the lepers," etc.), followed by another facsimile testimonial from Countess Tolstoy, Lady of Honour to Her Majesty the Empress of Russia, sent from the Winter Palace at St Petersburg ("our august Sovereign herself has deigned to give Miss Marsden proof of her sympathy," etc.). It isn't long before one realises that the whole book is thickly strewn with such letters of praise and recommendation: there is a letter from the wife of the Commander of all the Troops in Moscow; another from a certain Gregory Evereiff, Chief of the Tribe; another to "Our Loving Patroness Miss Marsden" from the lepers of Loutchinsky and Togouisky Nassleg, "written at their dictation and trans-lated into the Russian language by me—Yakut Government writer Vassiliy Nikolaeff Novine"; there is the text of a telegram, proudly re-printed, which reads, "VERY MANY THANKS FOR YOUR GOOD WISHES. HOPE YOU ARE GETTING ON WELL. EMPRESS"; and there are words of commendation from Florence Nightingale herself, the model and inspiration of all striving Victorian ladies bent on good works. At times the book reads like a roll of honour for all those who within a few years were swept away by death and revolution: Princess Natalie Shachovsky of Moscow; His Imperial Highness the Grand Duke Czarevitch; Vladimir, Bishop of Samara; Meletie, Bishop of Yakutsk; Prince Ivan Golitsyn, and many more. So eager was this strange and solitary Englishwoman to print these letters of respect and admiration from people in high places that one begins to wonder whether there might not have been some hidden motive behind their inclusion. Was she very unloved? Or did she fear that perhaps her readers might doubt the veracity of her account unless private testimonies of it were publicly posted up from chapter to chapter?

Certainly she struck an incredible figure at times. Over her undergarments of Jaeger wool, she says, she wore "a loose kind of body, lined with flannel, a very thickly-wadded eider-down ulster, with sleeves long enough to cover the hands entirely, the fur collar reaching high enough to cover the head and face. Then a sheep-skin reaching to the feet, and furnished with a collar which came over the fur one. Then over the sheep-skin . . . a *dacha*, which is a fur coat of reindeer skin." But this wasn't all, for she also had to put on "a long thick pair of Jaeger stockings made of long hair; over them a pair of gentlemen's thickest hunting stockings; over them a pair of Russian boots made of felt, coming high up over the knee; and over them a pair of brown felt *valenkies*. Then I was provided with a large fur bag or sack into which I could step." On her left arm she wore a badge of the Red Cross (she was a qualified nurse), and on her head a deerstalker she had bought in London; she carried a revolver, a whip and a little travelling bag slung over the shoulder. She was never, alas, very beautiful; but when she was accoutred for her Siberian journey she lost all femaleness entirely and assumed the form of an enormous bushy bear; in full costume she was, in fact, so heavy and immobile that she had to be lifted into her conveyance by three muscular policemen. Thus it was, fortified by a staple diet of English plum pudding, that she set out for the

outcast lepers of Yakutia and ultimately joined the thin but
distinguished ranks of female English eccentrics.

On February 1st, 1891, Kate Marsden, then aged nearly thirty-
two, left Moscow for Irkutsk. After three months' hard travelling,
mostly by sledge, she arrived; and after a further three weeks'
voyaging up the Lena she reached Yakutsk, the town that was to
be her headquarters. From here, with a cavalcade of fifteen men
and thirty horses, she set out on a journey of 2,000 miles through
Yakutia, a country which at the best of times is bloody to ride
through. Sitting astride a rude wooden saddle on a wild and
unbroken horse (she had never ridden in her life before), speaking no Russian but uplifted by the blessings of the local bishop,
she ventured into the great forest on her mission of succour,
driven on by a religious fervour and a desire for self-atonement
that sometimes seems to have come near to martyrdom mania.

Her narrative of this extraordinary journey is unrelievedly
harrowing; she narrowly escapes one disaster only to be confron-
ted with another; she endures unbelievable hardship and dangers,
and describes them all with undisguised relish. Following the
custom of travel writers of her time, Kate Marsden prefixes
every chapter with a résumé of its contents: "Sinking into
bogs—" she chirps in anticipation of chapter 8, "mosquito
torments begin—sleeping in a graveyard—bear alarms—frozen
corpses—depression." There is no respite in the next chapter:
"The lame, the halt and the blind—perils of the return journey—
alarms from bears and wild horses—stumbling onwards." Before
long she is promising the thrill of her own demise: "A weird
scene—a startling spectacle—the earth in flames—mad horses
and a narrow escape—a night of horrors—the doctor thinks I
need attention—in God's hands". No publicity man promoting
the latest Hollywood spine-chiller could have done better;
never before had Siberia been presented to genteel readers with
such hair-rising enthusiasm. If it was blood and thunder her
readers wanted, they got the thunder and they damned well nearly
got the blood.

But, though Kate Marsden chooses to describe only the most

hazardous and wearisome incidents on her travels, she does not unduly exaggerate them. In a summary of her experiences at the end of her book she gives a lugubriously fascinating picture of travel conditions in rural Yakutia that have changed hardly at all to the present day.

"When you are travelling through marshes in which your horse, without a moment's warning, sinks up to his stomach, you are obliged to hold on by the reins and by your knees and hands and every way, as best you can. The first ten marshes it was not so difficult; but after we had passed hundreds of them all the body ached; I felt as though I had spent fifty years on the tread-mill. It was then, that, to keep in the saddle, was a feat worthy of a hero.

"During the summer the mosquitoes are frightful, both in the night and in the day; and when you arrive at a yurt, which serves as a post-station, the dirt and vermin and smell are simply disgusting; bugs, lice, fleas, etc. cover the walls, as well as the benches on which you have to sleep. After a few days the body swells from their bites into a form that can neither be imagined nor described. They attack your eyes and your face, so that you would hardly be recognised by your dearest friend.

"The fatigue and the want of rest were dreadful. Cows and calves were in the same yurt with us, and the smell from them and from everything else was horrible. As there is only one yurt at a post-station, ladies and gentlemen are obliged to sleep all together, and any traveller that may be present at the same time; a gentleman might put up with it but it is impossible for a lady. After riding on horseback for the first time, my body was in constant pain, and complete rest with the possibility of undressing was indispensable; but as they say in French, "à la guerre comme à la guerre". As undressing was not possible I was obliged to rest the best way I could. To have even five minutes' rest we were obliged to have a fire made up of cowdung in this disgusting yurt, and, to prevent the smoke from escaping, as that is the only way to have any rest, we were obliged to cover the opening of the chimney. The mosquitoes left us alone; but as to our eyes, they were so irritated by the smoke that they were bathed in tears; and my head suffered even worse.

"Soon after we started on our journey, we were obliged to travel in the night, because our horses had no rest in the day time from the terrible horse-flies that were quite dangerous there. They instantly attacked the wretched beasts, so that it was an awful sight to see our horses with the blood running down their sides, many of them becoming so exhausted that they were not able to carry our luggage.

"At one place the bears might have attacked us with impunity. It was a very dangerous spot, as we were in the depths of a thick forest; we could hardly see two yards off, and the Yakuts saw eleven bears as we passed. Before starting, we all grasped our revolvers and guns, and we always had a large box filled with stones, which made a great clatter as we travelled; the bells also of some of our horses made a considerable noise. In the less dangerous parts of the forest everyone used to sing, making noise enough to frighten fifty bears. The horses are in such a fearful dread of the bears that they smell them afar off; and, as soon as they know they are near, they become almost unmanageable, dragging you through the forests, between the trees, flying like the wind. One thing was perfectly clear, that had the bears come near, it is quite certain some of us would have been killed, if not by the bears, then by the horses, who were almost mad.

"One further danger must be related, so that readers may have some notion of the many trials that had to be endured. After having left Viluisk one night we entered an immense forest, where the horses made a peculiar noise with their feet, as if they were walking over hollow ground. Having asked what it meant, I was told that we were near a place where the forest was burning. In about half an hour there was seen in the distance a small body of flames; but on getting nearer it seemed almost a picture of the infernal regions, so terrible was it to the sight, and yet we were obliged to go right into it. Far as could be seen there were flames and smoke rising from the ground, which was everywhere, apparently, burning. One of the Yakuts was in front;

I was next, my horse picking its way; but sometimes it would get into a hole where there was fire, when it became terrified, throwing itself from right to left, becoming restive and wild till one became almost exhausted; for, in addition to this, there was the effort to distinguish the path through the smoke with eyes smarting and almost blinded with the glare of the fire. However, we travelled on, but all at once we heard a dreadful noise behind us. Nothing could be seen through the flames and smoke, but the noise steadily kept coming nearer; our horses began to get still more restless and before we could have any idea where the sound came from, a horse with some luggage on it, mad with fright at the flames and the smoke, rushed into our midst. Mr Petroff, who was behind, had just time to give it a slash with his whip, which made it turn a little to the right, otherwise it would have been on me, and certainly I would have been killed. It was quite mad, and dashed right into the flames, as it was impossible to stop it, having so much to do to manage our own horses.

"This was the most terrible experience of the journey, and it was only through God's mercy that we were kept alive.

"Really, I think the sufferings of this journey have added twenty years to my age. But I would willingly do it ten times over to aid my poor lepers who are placed in the depths of these unknown forests."

I don't for a moment doubt the difficulties this remarkable woman had to contend with on her journey; nor do I doubt the admirable motives that urged her to go to the aid of the lepers, whose condition was undoubtedly horrible (I have spent a month in a leper colony myself). But what is very strange is her insistence, time and time again, on drawing attention to her heroism. Not content with describing her ordeal at length in the narrative, she includes two lengthy and often overlapping résumés of these same ordeals in the appendix, which she had written in French and asked a representative of the Governor of Yakutsk to sign as a witness of their veracity. Why did she feel so obliged to prove her case so often, to convince the world of all she had endured in this noble cause? Did she want to boost the sales of her book? Did she fear her story would be discredited when she returned home? Or did she (and I suspect she did) wish to leave no doubt in anybody's mind that these were the deeds of a woman who by her own sufferings had assumed the sufferings of others and by her own self-sacrifice had imitated the ultimate sacrifice of Him whom she loved, Jesus Christ, and attained to saintliness?

Whatever it was, it did her no good. Doubts *were* cast on her veracity as a traveller; by some she was even considered to be insane (a few years before her Siberian journey she had suffered a nervous breakdown). In 1921, to put an end to the persecution she claimed had dogged her, she wrote a second book, *My Mission to Siberia: A Vindication.* In a sense, though, no vindication was needed, for as a result of her work a hospital *was* built for the lepers of Yakutsk, staffed by nuns and financed by her own writings and funds she had raised in Russia, Britain and America. She may not have achieved the special recognition she sought but *that* mission, at least, had been accomplished.

Kate Marsden died in 1931 but her ghost still walks the wooden streets of Yakutsk, her spiritual home; one can almost see her, gleefully obdurate in a balloon of furs, aching her way along on the back of a bleeding, bow-legged horse; and nightly still, I imagine, her spirit is invoked by our earnest friend, the Museum curator. I hope he finishes his book, and lays Miss Kate's poor soul.

.   .   .

It would be wrong to imagine that such a breed of women has vanished entirely. The age of lady eccentrics may be over but there are still many who are willing to invade men's provinces with their own brand of tough single-mindedness. It was in Yakutsk that I first heard of Larisca Popougaeva, for example, a young woman from Leningrad who has become a heroine among the Russians. In 1954, as a member of a team of geological prospectors which was itself headed by another woman, she parachuted into the virgin forest to the north of Yakutsk. Abandoned there, she spent most of the long summer days crawling on her belly among the swamps and knotted tree roots, a little geological hammer in one hand and a notebook in the other. Life wasn't easy. Several previous geological survey teams had come near to disaster in this inclement region. In 1926, one of them, in danger of starvation in the gold-bearing region of Aldan, found the necessities of life were at such a premium that for a tumbler of salt they had to pay half a tumbler of gold, and every kilogram of meat cost forty grams of gold. But the girl survived. At the end of four rugged months she was picked up and brought back to Yakutsk. There she reported that she had stumbled on some pipes of pure kimberlite, which promised the presence of a vast diamond field whose ores would yield more than those of South Africa. She was not mistaken. To-day the diamond mines of Mirny, among the biggest in the world, are one of the Soviet Union's most valuable mineral assets.

As a result of the work of people like Larisca Popougaeva, Siberia, not long ago almost the least-explored region on earth, has now been mapped across its entire length and breadth and down to a depth of 10,000 feet. New mineral deposits are discovered with monotonous regularity (nearly a hundred were reported in 1964) and Siberia, in natural resources among the richest regions on earth, is fast becoming the heart of the Soviet Union.

Naturally we wanted to see some of these new-found riches with our own eyes. We asked Charlie Chan if we could go to the diamond mines, but he said no, the airstrip was inoperable because of the thaw, we would have to go to the goldfields of Aldan instead. We said we didn't want to go to Aldan. We told him that, while we were quite certain that the goldfields there were large, productive, efficient and up-to-date, we had nevertheless been assured on the best authority that they were, from a photographic point of view, as dull as sin. We wouldn't go.

Charlie Chan was startled. "Not go?" he murmured. "Not go to Aldan?" The spanner jingled in the works; vexation throbbed in our yellow friend's head. "We'll see about that," he threatened, and left abruptly.

"I think," mused John after he had gone, "that Moscow will be hearing about this little counter-revolution shortly."

Thus, under threat of immediate recall, we went down to dinner and wondered where we would land up next.

9

An Expedition towards the Arctic Sea

EVERY day Yakutsk had been growing warmer. The last fragments of ice in the pools melted; the frozen soil thawed down to
a foot or more and turned the dirt roads into quagmires; the
chilly north wind died down a little and sometimes the grey
clouds parted and let through a few warm rays of sunshine.
Springtime was hurtling towards midsummer with characteristic
Siberian precipitateness; there was no real night any longer, only
a brief twilight that settled silently over the town like a coma;
and in our hotel room we could now afford to leave the three-
paned, doubly-insulated windows open. Out of town, down
by the Lena escarpment, the river was flowing freely where only
a few days before it had streamed with a flotsam of broken ice;
poppies were already blooming on the green-brown grassy banks,
and among the scattered clumps of stunted alders and Arctic
willows clouds of mosquitoes—enormous carnivores that settled
thickly over every inch of exposed skin—hummed loudly for
blood in dense, gyrating columns.

We sat on a gentle slope overlooking the river, away from
the places where the mosquitoes were for the moment confined.
Below us an arm of the Lena idled its way towards the northern
ocean; on either side of us stretched the forest-crested escarpment that delineated the ancient banks of the river. Temporarily
absent from the clutches of Charlie Chan and the telephone line
to Moscow, enjoying the illusion of freedom that the prospect of
this wide valley and the enormous sky gave us, we breathed deeply
of the clean air from the hills and relaxed.

"Of course you are seeing Yakutsk at the wrong time of the

year," Niki the cameraman was saying. "Now it is neither one thing nor the other. The early spring is a messy time. Everything looks scruffy."

"When is the best time, then?" I asked.

"There are many beautiful days in winter. The Siberian winter isn't as bad as people make out. It's cold, yes, but it's dry and there are many still, clear days. It's very lovely then. One feels good. The clearness of the light is astonishing, and so are the colours—such beautiful pastel colours. You should come here then. The snow is blue, everything is clean and fresh, everything glitters. And so silent—you can hear the squeak of sledge-runners on the snow two kilometres away."

"You're not looking forward to the summer, then?" John asked.

"But of course I am. I'm just saying the Siberian winter can be a good time. It can also be a terrible time. The cold pole of the earth is in Yakutia. At Verkkoyansk the temperature has dropped as low as −71°C. (−95°F.). And in the summer it's as hot as Trinidad on the equator—more than 37°C. (100°F.). That's a temperature difference of nearly 150°C. (200°F.). There's no more extreme climate in the world."*

"Is it true," I asked, "that your breath makes a crackling sound when it freezes."

"Yes, it does sometimes. We have a story here that if you shout to a friend across a broad river and he can't hear you it's because all the words have frozen in the air. But when the spring comes all the words thaw out and if you go back there then you can hear everything you said six months ago."

I imagined a valley full of the cacophony of old words, the air ringing with questions, abuse and laughter and no one within miles. I imagined stalking the wintry wastes with a stove and a box of matches and lighting them up at deserted encampments and hearing last year's jokes and last year's gossip melt about my ears. Winter, the Yakut's tape-recorder . . .

*Oimyakon, not far away, claims an even lower temperature of −82°C. (−115°F.) This is the lowest temperature recorded in the northern hemisphere. The lowest recorded temperature in the world −87°C. (−125°F.) was recorded in the Antarctic.

"When winter gets very cold," Niki continued, "it's best not to go out. Your nostrils can be blocked with ice and your whole body becomes as stiff as a board. In less than ten hours the frost will penetrate the thickest furs to the skin. And it's funny how ice can burn. Best to light a big fire and sit by it. Not that the winter holds things up very much. Work still goes on. Children still go to school . . . "

Just then a very familiar sound floated across the valley—familiar yet strange and unexpected in this place. The summer cuckoo was back in the land of the cold pole, putting the winter to rout, usurping the nest.

Niki stood up. "If I were you," he said, "I'd go up north. There's still a bit of winter left up there. And if you want to see wolves and reindeers and things like that, now's the time. The reindeers have been dropping their young and the wolf packs have moved in to try and get the calves. That would make good film."

.   .   .

When we got back to Yakutsk we told Charlie Chan we wanted to go north.

"North," he said, vacantly. "North? Why north? Where north?"

"North," we said, "just anywhere north. We're not particular."

Charlie looked at us, from one to the other. A mask of inscrutability was pulled across his face; it hid, I am sure, a brain ticking like a time-bomb. Had we asked the impossible? He turned on his heels and departed. Half-way through the door he looked back at us.

"You'll regret it!" he exclaimed, and giggled.

After he had gone we sat down and composed a post-card. It has long been an English custom to notify the editor of *The Times* of an annual event of some importance. We could not, as the only Englishmen who had observed this event in latitude 129′E., longitude 62′N., fail to do the same.

"*Dear Sir,*" we wrote,

    "*We have just heard the first cuckoo of spring.*

"Yours faithfully,
   J. Bayliss
   D. Botting
Yakutsk, E. Siberia. 4th June."

Had we foreseen the acute embarrassment this simple message would cause us when we returned to Moscow, we would never have sent it. But we despatched it on its 5,000-mile journey, hoping it might lighten the day of some jaded journalist in distant E.C.4., and when Charlie Chan returned we forgot about it.

He held in his hand two air-tickets. He seemed happy. He even laughed.

"In a few hours' time," he said, "we are catching a plane to Nizhnye Kresty. That is in the north. In fact, I would go as far as to say that it is about as far north as you can reasonably expect to get. Nizhnye Kresty is on the edge of the Arctic Ocean. Are you ready?"

⠀⠀⠀⠀⠀•⠀⠀⠀•⠀⠀⠀•

We left the hotel at half-past two to the sound of morning cock-crow. A blood-red, swollen sun hung low over the town like some unnatural portent, and the wooden houses along the road, silent and shuttered, seemed to skulk in the indigo twilight of a premature dawn.

The airport building was crowded with Yakut and Russian peasantry and the air inside was stale and fetid. Fathers queued at a small buffet counter for what refreshments there were to be had, while their children lay on sacks and bundles, stiffened in sleep as if in an agony of death. The smell and the congestion of sleepy, boorish bodies was again too much for us; we were forced into the cold outside and sat on our film boxes watching the great sun lumber up into the sky; we warmed ourselves at it as if in front of a fire.

At four we were herded on to the plane, a four engined IL-18. It was a non-service flight; that is to say, we had to carry all our baggage on to the plane ourselves and stow it as best we could; there were no refreshments to be had, not even tea, either on the plane itself or at the places where we landed. This was bad

enough, but we had not been airborne for long before it was evident that the nauseating stench peculiar to any confined assembly
of Yakuts was slowly asserting itself; the smell seemed worse
at the back, where we sat, and was accompanied by a rising—and
before long almost unendurable—temperature, as if the highly-
spiced Yakut breath was simultaneously undergoing the processes
of fermentation and combustion. I felt as if I was being slowly
boiled in a hop vat. To make matters worse, the lavatory was
situated immediately behind us; once the aircraft had gained its
ceiling and levelled off, our fellow-voyagers made frequent and
haphazard use of it, and the troubling smell that issued from this
ill-used cubicle made the atmosphere of the plane even more insufferable. "One day," John said, turning to me and holding his
nose with his fingers, "when I'm a great, fat, nasty capitalist,
I'm going to come back to this country with a crate full of air-
fresheners, and I'm going to make a great, fat, nasty, old fortune."

I looked out of the window. Snowy white hills rolled away
to the north; the forest was thinning out and now the brown,
leafless trees were more scattered, occurring only in clumps or
in narrow belts along the banks of the frozen rivers; before long
the great Siberian taiga had almost disappeared, giving way to the
bare hills and the flat plains that slope down towards the tundra
and the sea. There were no roads or signs of human life in those
northern wilds beneath us. This was the Siberian desert and
where we were going was one of its remotest oases.

After two hours the plane began to dip towards the earth.
We had completed half our journey and reached a latitude close to
the Arctic Circle. Out of a cloudless and brilliantly blue sky
we descended to an earthen strip at the edge of a small township
and landed, appropriately, in complete ignorance as to our whereabouts. Already we were lost and swallowed up in the enormity
of this land.

We stepped out of the plane and wandered towards the wooden
hut at the edge of the airfield perimeter. Never before or since,
I think, have I been so overwhelmed and exhilarated by the
sense of space this wide landscape gave me. Far away there were

ranges of hills, rising gently behind each other, receding endlessly away in the clear, pellucid light of that early Arctic morning;
far from confining the expanse of the visible world around us,
they seemed to extend it with a promise of infinity, as if beyond
them there might be glittering plains leading without hindrance
to the edge of the world. As I looked around me in the crisp,
crystalline sunlight, I felt a curious expansion of the spirit,
a sense of freedom peculiar to deserts, and I breathed deeply
of the delicious, lager-cool air and felt refreshed.

I wish I could have said the same for my stomach. I was hungry
and abominably dry. I dearly longed for a hot coffee to wet my throat.
Along with John and Charlie Chan and all the other passengers,
we stormed the airport hut, put our heads round every door,
inspected every room, circumambulated the entire building
and found nothing that resembled a buffet or a tea-stall; there
was nothing to be had and no one to complain to except the
peasants who lay sprawled asleep along the bare boards inside the
hut or against the wooden walls outside. Disconsolate, we waited
for the plane to take off again and slapped at the mosquitoes
that now began to whine about our heads.

Nizhnye Kresty is in the furthest north-east corner of Yakutia
and is nearer to the United States of America than it is to Yakutsk.
We still had nearly two hours of flying-time ahead of us and as
we droned steadily north up the Kolyma river and crossed the
Arctic Circle the world below grew progressively more desolate
and snow-covered. Before the advent of the aeroplane, this
journey had to be undertaken in sledges pulled by horses, reindeers
or dogs and it took four very arduous and exhausting months
to complete. This was hardly surprising. Even from the aloof
altitude of the plane I could see it was a terrain that was decidedly
inimical to man; innumerable rivers and streams traversed it
and though the countless thousands of circular lakes spattered
across the tundra were frozen now, in the summer they must
present an almost insuperable barrier to the land traveller.
Even so, I longed to descend. There is in most of us still some
remnant of our ancient nomadic instinct, that occasional

anarchic urge to strike camp and wander on; it is an instinct
which is stimulated and at the same time frustrated by air travel,
so that in time the vision of the seemingly boundless, primeval
and virgin earth below becomes almost unbearably tantalising
and one yearns to get out and feel the rude earth under one's feet
and the wind in one's face and set one's course wherever one
pleases across the wide world. I wasn't sorry when we started our
descent towards Nizhnye Kresty and nosed down towards the
frozen Kolyma; I caught sight of an expanse of blue sea as the
plane banked, and white islands rising from the sea and ships still
ice-locked in the river; I saw a collection of huts and an earthen
runway glistening in the brilliant light, and then we had touched
down alongside the river and the engines were roaring in
reverse.

Charlie Chan turned to us. "*Tak!*" he said simply. "So!"
And he gave a jibbering, simian laugh. I don't think he liked
flying.

.   .   .

Winter had passed through Nizhnye like a war. Now, in the
peacetime of the spring, the inhabitants had emerged from their
shelters to survey the battered town and pick among the ruins.
During the nine months of winter the people of Nizhnye had
jettisoned their waste into the streets outside their homes—there
was nowhere else to put it, for the river was frozen and the
ground was ice-covered and hard as iron, and in any case it was
soon hidden by the snow. But now in the thaw the snow had gone,
leaving the rubbish of the winter's siege exposed in the squelching
mud throughout the town; at every turn one came across piles
of food cans and all the discarded bric-à-brac of human existence—
an old boot, a sodden mattress, a child's broken toy, a light bulb,
a smashed guitar—randomly strewn like the blast-blown litter
of an artillery bombardment; almost one expected to see a child's
hand poking through the debris, a shattered femur sticking out
of the mud. The wooden houses of this small settlement, perched
on the right bank near the mouth of the Kolyma, had been
scarred by prolonged exposure to ice and wind; some leaned at

crazy angles, a few had been ripped apart; the wooded sidewalks were broken and warped. Nizhnye Kresty at the end of winter looked like a ghost town, a decayed town on a dissolving mound of detritus from some earlier habitation; only the specialised equipment with which the Russians fought their Arctic winters — the caterpillar-tracked tractors, the trucks with massive balloon tyres ringed with chains, the logs lashed together as huge sledges — gave any indication that the war had not passed through Nizhnye without a struggle.

It was June 5th and still the river was frozen; the ocean-going tankers that had been caught by the freeze-up in early September were still, after nine months, firmly held in the grip of the ice. But any day now the ice was expected to break up. Already it was moving, stirred by the force of the submarine currents that flowed beneath it; from time to time I could hear it groan and crack; once I saw a thin fissure flicker from the bank like a fork of lightning; as I watched, the ice would seem to bloom with tongues of fire as one loosened floe ground against another and forced up a coronet of glistening splinters.

Not so long ago, when the region of Kolyma round Nizhnye Kresty was officially registered as "unfit for human habitation", the annual break-up of the river was a life or death affair. In those days the population survived the winter on stocks of frozen fish, but by March their stores were often finished and they would be forced to eat food usually given to the dogs — fishbones, entrails and half-rotten herring. By May they would be eating boiled leather leggings and straps and dried fish skins (normally used instead of glass for the windows of the houses), and the dogs would be eating each other. Under such circumstances any unusual delay in the melting of the river could result in widespread starvation. Between May 28th and June 14th, when all food had gone and the fishing places were covered with ice and driftwood brought down from the upper part of the river, life was difficult. "Everywhere," wrote an eye-witness, "one saw famine-swollen, livid faces, with fever-bright eyes from which despair looked out."

How much things have changed in such a short time. To-day Nizhnye Kresty is supplied by plane and ship with every necessity. In the Aeroflot staff mess, where we at last broke our fast, we were treated to one of the best meals we ever had in the Soviet Union. Our table was piled high with fresh white bread, lashings of butter, glasses of deliciously cool kvas, ham, cold fish, fish soup, meat stew and cheese, and we were asked—pleaded with, even—to eat as much as we liked and ask for more if we wanted it. It will be a long time before I forget the spontaneous, unbounded delight of the two Russian women who tended us. In the three years they had been here (their husbands were Aeroflot pilots based at Nizhnye) they had never seen a foreigner. Possibly, they said, none had come here in this century until we arrived. Their affection, their utter joy in having us was marvellous. They sat with us at our table and prattled away. Were we married? No? We would soon find wives on Nizhnye. There were girls here who would gobble us up, they said. One had to go a long way in the Soviet Union to find good home cooking and an uninhibited reception such as this. The further one went, it seemed, the better the food, and the nicer the people. It was worth it, even if it did mean venturing to the edge of the Arctic Ocean and a lonely spot on exactly the opposite side of the globe from home.

Later that afternoon we went with Charlie Chan to a wooden hut that housed the local government office. Here we were introduced to the local Party President (in England we would call him a Mayor) and the Director of the local Sovkhoz (a reindeer collective). These two little earnest, nervous, Eskimo-like gentlemen seemed to be in charge of our visit; it was up to them, I gathered, what arrangements should be made following our unexpected arrival in their town. We sat down in the President's office, round a long table covered in green baize, and began the only commercial negotiation we ever encountered during all our time in the Soviet Union. To go into the tundra, they explained, we would need a helicopter. Did we realise how much a helicopter would cost? No, we said, we didn't. 600 roubles, they said, there and back, petrol included. 600 roubles came to about £200 at our rate of exchange. We protested. We said that though this price might seem reasonable to them, to us it was absurd. We couldn't possibly afford it. They conferred among themselves. Charlie Chan was enjoying himself immensely. 300 roubles, they said, they wanted to help, they didn't want to be mean. No, we said, they didn't understand, we came from England, not America, we didn't have that much money. Again the conference amongst themselves in their strange, Yakutian tongue; again the quietly proffered compromise. Do you think, they asked, you could afford sixty roubles and the cost of the provisions? That all depends, we said craftily, on the cost of the provisions. Two crates of brandy, Charlie Chan said, rather too promptly, and a salami sausage. So we agreed and everyone was happy. It was an excellent bargain, for in England a helicopter would have cost ten times that amount. One thing puzzled us, though. If they were happy to hire their helicopter for sixty roubles, who would have got the money if they had hired it for 600?

The helicopter was due at noon the next day. It would deposit us in the tundra at some spot along the Arctic sea-board where the reindeer people would be camped with their herds, and it would leave us for a few days before returning to pick us up. In the meantime, the President suggested, we should try and get some sleep, since our stay in the tundra might well be strenuous.

Sleep, however, looked an unlikely proposition, for it soon became apparent that the sun was not going to set. Even after our evening meal it was still high in the sky and Nizhnye Kresty was as well lit as at noon. Neither of us had ever experienced this northern phenomenon of endless daylight, nor the havoc it causes in the body's time mechanism; we wandered restlessly about the town, disturbed by a feeling of nature gone awry, of a world become out of joint; we were as active as battery hens stimulated by an artificial lamp in the night. Our room in the local hostel didn't help. There were no curtains to pull across the windows and the light poured cheerily in. The old hands had pulled their beds out into the windowless corridors and even on to the dark landing at the top of the stairs; there in the dimmer parts of the building they were able at last to fall asleep, and the entire hostel rumbled with the snores of communal slumber. For us there was no such simple solution and we sat disconsolately on the edge of our iron-framed beds until, towards midnight, the sun reddened and dipped towards the river. At about one in the morning it looked as if it would finally sneak over the horizon and relinquish the world to a blessed and belated darkness; already the clear, bright sky had paled through the colours of jade, sapphire and citrine, and now it was flushed with a furious crimson whose reflection turned the river of ice into a river of fire; every splinter, every upturned fang of ice across the encrusted Kolyma flickered in that bonfire light like tongues of flame; the river looked like the glowing lava-flow of an erupting volcano.

But the sun never set; it hung momentarily low over the horizon and then, minute by minute, crept, like a balloon that had discharged its ballast, higher into the sky. At one o'clock there had been a sort of sunset; thirty minutes later there was a sort of dawn. By two it was full daylight again and the dogs were yelping in the streets outside. I slept as best I could, a blanket pulled over my head to keep out that terrible, prying, remorseless light, my slumber disturbed by bouts of wakefulness and maniac dreams. I dreamt I was cleaning my teeth on an ice floe when a small tug steamed by and hove-to when it saw me. Christopher Columbus leaned over the rail and said to me, "I am looking for America. I'm told it's here or hereabouts." "I'm afraid I can't help you," I replied, "my visa's only good for another week." Just then the sea froze round Columbus's ship and soon he, John and I, with the unquestioned logic and mobility of dreams, were in India, sipping long whiskies in a kind of patio, where Charlie Chan joined us and said, "I'd like you to meet my wife, the Maharanee of Mysore." "How do you do," we all chanted in chorus. Then there was a loud roaring sound, a splintering crack like an explosion, and as I woke I knew Columbus's ship was being ground to pieces by the ice.

I staggered to the window. The river was breaking up. There

was another deafening boom similiar to the one which had, presumably, wakened me. Somewhere lower down the river an ice dam had given way and the course to the sea was open. The river was on the move; the ice was being ripped apart; long chasms opened up across its breadth and with startling swiftness, like the shattering of a car's windscreen, the frozen surface split into innumerable fragments. Slowly the ice floes sidled away from the bank, were caught up by the current and glided inexorably out of sight. Swept up in this funereal procession were entire trees, shrubs, empty petrol cans, the stiffened corpse of a dog and the battered hulk of a small boat. The river was being cleansed by the enema of the thaw, swept clear of the flotsam of an age-old winter.

"She is moving, our little mother Kolyma," the natives would exclaim in years gone by as they crowded the banks to watch this annual, all-important event. "How she suffers, our little mother Kolyma," they lamented as the ice cracked and groaned. Even to-day it is a momentous occasion, this definitive manifestation of the earth's natural cycle; the world that had died in September is born again in June; man, helpless and moved, looks on at the birth in wonder.

As I watched the pancakes of ice drift north to the sea, I became conscious that the river's break-up was not the only thing that had happened that fine morning. An awful stench began to fill the room. It woke John.

"Holy-moses-and-mother-of-god," he mumbled. "What's that?"

I had a strong suspicion what it was. I opened the door. The smell from downstairs swept in like a plague.

"I think," I said, "that the lavatory has melted."

It had, as before very long we were obliged to find out. The lavatories in the hostel were simply holes in the ground that dropped to a deep pit below. There was no sewerage in Nizhnye but in the winter this didn't matter—the sub-zero temperatures normally kept everything as sweet and fresh as laundered linen. But now in the thaw . . . !

We dressed hurriedly and went out to the Aeroflot mess for a breakfast of coffee and curds. Afterwards we went to the quartermaster's stores to be kitted out for our impending journey.

The quartermaster, a stubby man in a smart, grey Aeroflot uniform, surveyed us expertly. He measured the circumference of our heads, examined the size of our feet, calculated our resistance to cold. From shelves piled high with all sorts of polar clothing he pulled articles that he thought might fit us. One by one we tried them on: a fur hat, two pairs of thick knee-length woollen stockings, a pair of quilted, padded trousers, a pair of tall felt boots, a polo-necked sweater and a blue kapok-lined jacket with an anorak hood. Thus attired, we emerged into the brilliant warm sunshine of mid-morning and sweated our way back to the hostel to pack; the shirt-sleeved inhabitants of Nizhnye cast side-long glances at our clumsy and voluminously wrapped forms, and wondered. We wondered, too. Did we really have to set off disguised as Soviet airmen on a survival exercise? Apparently we did. Charlie Chan, when he came to collect us as departure-time drew near, was also warmly garbed. Though the river was melting here, out there it must still be very cold.

The helicopter was waiting for us at the airfield. It was a KA-18, a large, general purpose craft, with a single engine and twin rotors. Besides John, Charlie and myself, there were a crew of five and the Party President, the Sovkhoz Director, the Sovkhoz Deputy-Director and the President of the Local Trade Union on board. We exchanged greetings and clambered into the helicopter. The door was firmly shut; the rotor blades whirled; they roared as they accelerated to the correct number of revolutions, and the dust swirled. Gently we lifted into the air and headed towards the north-west.

For a short while we flew above the river, then turned away and crossed its left bank, aiming for the startlingly empty spaces beyond. It was as if someone had switched a light off, for the glaring whiteness of the river-ice gave way to the sombre brown of the marshy tundra, from whose flooded bogs shot occasional blinding flashes of reflected sunlight. Behind us now was the thin line of stunted trees along the Kolyma's bank—the only sizeable vegetation in the entire territory; ahead was a featureless waste of lichen, moss and sedge, where nothing grew larger than an occasional, miserable bush.

At a speed of seventy m.p.h. and a height of 100 feet, we sped on. We must have been heading in a northerly direction, for we soon passed the furthest frontier of the thaw and the tundra became snow-covered again. Sometimes we came down low, as if to have a closer look at some clue to the whereabouts of the reindeer people we were searching for; sometimes we banked and swept round in a great arc. From time to time the Director of the Nizhnye Sovkhoz, a member of one of the local aboriginal tribes, shouted instructions to the pilot or peered at the horizon through his field-glasses. After an hour or so it was clear that we were lost.

We were lost in a white desert whose limitlessness rivalled any conventional sand desert I had ever seen. Its very sameness exaggerated the sweep of its horizon; one could imagine, without having to see, the hundreds of identical, barren, snowy miles beyond the dead flat line that divided earth from sky; a single glance could encompass the infinity of the north. Then we saw something that broke the monotony of the level, unchanging tundra; like castaways who had spotted a plume of smoke rising from a hitherto deserted ocean, we all looked at it, were grateful for it. The pilot promptly set course towards it.

It was a *bulganniakh*. In English we would call it (for what it is worth) a pingo, an ice-cored swelling rising like a conical hill from the plain, a large frost boil eroded by wind and weather into the shape of a rounded pyramid. We flew towards it like a migratory bird seeking the refuge of a light-house; rising a few hundred feet above the marshes, it promised a firm, dry landing spot and an elevated vantage point from which we could survey the surrounding landscape and take fresh bearings. We reached it, nosed round it, fluttered down towards its summit, and landed with infinite delicacy on its pelt of coarse grass.

.   .   .

It was four o'clock in the afternoon and we had been flying for nearly two hours. The sky was a bright cobalt blue and the air was warm; far above our heads circled a wild white swan whose honking cries broke the great silence, Charlie Chan shot at it with his twelve-bore, and missed, and after it had gone there was no sound of any living creature, nor a breath of wind. The pilot of the helicopter clambered on to the top of his machine and sat on one of the rotor blades, surveying the empty tundra that stretched all around us and far away. But he saw nothing—no landmark. no movement, no clue.

"*Nichevo*," he said with a shrug. "Not to worry." He conferred with the Nizhnye officials and they pointed to different quarters of the horizon and argued over a map full of blank unnamed spaces. Somewhere in all those miles of snowy wilderness there was a migrating reindeer herd and a little camp of herdsmen. They moved along a precise, seasonal route. But where was that route?

We flew on for another two hours and landed four more times. We circled and soared, dropped close to the earth, and tacked like a yacht. Then the Captain shouted to us from his cabin and I squeezed my face against the porthole and saw, 200 feet beneath us and silhouetted against the snow, the nursery figments of my childhood dreams. A herd of some 500 head of reindeer, panic-stricken by the juddering roar of the helicopter, were galloping at full stretch across the tundra. My mind's eye clicked like a camera-shutter and for a moment the reindeer were frozen in mid-gallop; clearly etched against the snow, they seemed like creatures from a pre-historic cave-painting, or like an animal frieze carefully scratched on a bone. I blinked, and they galloped on, charging crazily across the plain until we had left them far behind.

We were getting near. Soon we were approaching a huddle of grey wigwams. Tiny, furry figures emerged to stare up at us as we hovered above them. Then we were descending into the land of the Chukchi tribe.

The helicopter settled to the ground and the engines died. The door was opened.

"Lordy me," John said, staring out in disbelief. "Hiawatha himself."

I looked out, into the weather-worn face of a Stone Age man, a short nervous Chukchi, clad from head to toe in skins. He was, I learnt later, Afanasi the Brigadier, the foreman in charge of the reindeer herd. A nice man, but a bit of a shock at first sight.

The sun had disappeared behind cloud now and a bitter north wind blew from the sea; even in our winter clothing we shivered. Crew and passengers hastily unloaded stores from the helicopter and began to erect a tent, a double-walled, igloo-shaped structure of black, windproof cloth, with a little chimney in the top and a glass porthole in the side. This was to be our home for the next few days, and into it we carried camp beds and sleeping bags, guns, ammunition, two crates of brandy and a salami sausage. That, it seemed, represented the sum total of our equipment.

We stooped into the tent, out of the wind. The sky was darkening and shortly it began to snow—tiny, damp, driving flakes. Thirteen of us, including the reindeer "brigadier", sat hunched round the walls of the circular tent. One brandy crate was placed in the middle to serve as a table; the other crate was opened and the first of the two dozen bottles we had brought with us was uncorked. The bottle was passed around.

"This is the life!" the helicopter captain sighed, wiping the mouth of the bottle with his sleeve. He had seen service in the Antarctic. For him this was a picnic, a fortuitous day off in pleasant rural surroundings.

It seemed that the others thought the same. They opened another bottle. Outside the wind was beginning to howl.

"Although it's not exactly *me*," John said, "what I'd really like is a nice cup of tea."

"Cognac?" Charlie Chan enquired, grimacing in a parody of bonhomie as he offered us the bottle.

Just then a mummified looking figure appeared in the entrance and held back the tent flap with a skeletal paw. She was so old that her face was grooved like a withered walnut; exposed to a lifetime of wind and frost, she had been worn away like a natural object, a piece of driftwood on the beach, or an old shell. Her skin was as dry and cracked as ancient parchment, and the northern climate had tanned it to a deep ruddy brown. Like a leathery lizard she stood, bent almost double, peering in. She clutched a saucepan of steaming meat in her free hand and with this she advanced into the middle of the tent. This was the brigadier's mother, so old no one could guess the year of her birth or how many winters had passed since she had first travelled the bleak wastes of her homeland. She was clad in skins, and when she spoke her voice was like the rustling of dead leaves. She was terrifying.

The brigadier took the saucepan from her and the old woman creaked out of the tent into the evening gale. A reindeer had been specially killed for us and its flesh had been boiled to make a banquet in honour of our arrival; each of us in turn selected some unchoice morsel from the pan and gnawed at the rubbery meat. What was left at the end was taken away. We would see it again, no doubt, at breakfast.

At length the crewmen and the Party President and the Sovkhoz Director stood up to take their departure. They boarded the helicopter and quickly it ascended into the grey sky and turned for home. Reluctantly we uncorked another brandy bottle. Our stay in the Siberian tundra had begun.

· · ·

Alone among the aboriginal tribes of northern Siberia, the Chukchi offered some resistance to the early Russian pioneers who came to subdue and exploit them. The Yakuts, the Samoyeds, the Tungus, the Koryaks, the Lamuts, the Yukagirs, the Ostiaks and other tribal groups who have now ceased to exist made little defence against the new invaders of their territories; they were maligned, maltreated and held for nothing; after centuries of marginal living they were reduced to an even more pitiable condition, and in time their numbers were annually decimated. But the Chukchi were made of sterner stuff. They would not give in.

They fell upon the Cossack bands and Russian colonists with spears and lances and stolen flintlocks. When attacked themselves, they died bravely. After nearly two hundred years of dogged in-fighting, they obtained from the Russians an acknowledgement of their right to co-existence; an uneasy truce reigned.

The Russians came to respect these little, primitive people. They respected their toughness and independence, their honesty and industry. They left them, more or less, to themselves. But the Russians had brought with them to Siberia three terrible weapons—smallpox, syphilis and vodka—against which the Chukchi had no defence. By the end of the last century their population had dwindled to less than 3,000. Epidemics of small-pox carried off hundreds of them at a time; whole camps rotted with tertiary syphilis; the survivors would sell precious furs and the winter's fish store for a bottle of the traders' vodka, and they would drink themselves, ultimately, to death.

Where once, according to a Chukchi legend, "there were more hearth fires on the shores of the Kolyma than there are stars in the sky", there was now only a handful of sickened, starving savages. Though they hunted seals and walruses in the sea, fished in the rivers, trapped furs, snared wildfowl and bred reindeer, their nomadic life was wretched in the extreme. Often they had to invent a thousand ways of starving to death when their staple food of frozen raw fish gave out. They would eat the bark of trees, catch field rats or extract undigested vege-tation from the intestines of reindeers; instead of tea, they drank a decoction of red bilberries, and smoked suede leather cut into strips. They knew nothing of bread, or money, or soap; they were obliged to do without salt, and, since they had no linen, they were forced to wear their furs next to their naked skin; the only way they could make a fire was by friction and they used their own urine to wash in. Like Eskimoes (to whom they are closely related), the Chukchi would kill off their old people when times were particularly hard, and to both neighbours and strangers they readily offered their wives and daughters in amiable prostitution, for usually they had few other comforts to give. During the brief, eight-week summer, they made love, and gorged themselves on fish, and on berries boiled in deer fat; in winter they starved, and their children died by the score. A Chukchi adult did well to live beyond 35.

Such a state of affairs lasted to well within the memory of many Chukchi living to-day. But in 1923 their territory was declared a Soviet province and in the years that followed a new regime was enforced. It followed the familiar pattern of Soviet rule over backward minority groups. In the first place, national self-respect had to be restored among the Chukchi as among other aboriginal tribes. In some cases their names were changed, and in this way the Samoyeds (which means "cannibals") became known as Nentsi, the Tungus became Yevenki and the Chukchi themselves were re-styled Luoravetlans—a name which does not appear to have stuck. At the same time, the simple cultures of these tribes were reinstated to their full dignity; philologists prepared grammars of their languages and invented alphabets for them; a literacy programme was inaugurated, and any aboriginal with literary gifts was published by the local national press; poets emerged hot-foot, so to speak, from the Stone Age.

The second task of the Soviets was to give these people a satisfactory material basis for existence, in order to raise their appalling living standards and put an end to famine and disease. To this end the principles of collectivisation were applied to the hitherto individualistic and random occupations of hunting and herding. Modern and adequate provisions and equipment were provided for the Chukchi, and a veterinary service was set up. Many of the nomads were settled in permanent villages where there were schools, clinics, co-operative stores and bath-houses, and where they could learn the skills of the mechanic and the builder. Slowly and surely they were led into the modern world and persuaded to abandon their superstitions and shamans for the progressive ideologies of Soviet socialism.

Today the Chukchi are the great reindeer herders of the USSR and the Arctic. The herds are prospering (the target of the current Seven-Year Plan is one million head) and their traditional enemies, the wolves and the warble fly, are being exterminated. The Chukchi themselves have quadrupled their population and there are now 13,000 of them living in their own national district of Chukotka, east of the Kolyma.

Even so, it was difficult to see the working life of our Chukchi host, Afanasi the Brigadier, in terms of a Sovkhoz. Everything about it cried out from the past rather than the present or the future. The simple, double-walled wigwams of reindeer hide that constituted Afanasi's camp probably hadn't changed in design for hundreds, possibly thousands of years; nor had their clothing or their diet of reindeer meat and reindeer milk. The seasonal pattern of their lives was the same as it had always been; towards the beginning of winter, in August or early September, they would leave the tundra and move south towards the taiga where the reindeer could scrape moss from the snow along the forest fringe; in the spring, to escape the hordes of mosquitoes, they would move back through the tundra again, travelling fifteen kilometres a day on a wide circling migration.

But things *have* changed. Afanasi, as foreman of a herd of 2,800 head, was getting paid a salary of 350 roubles a month—a figure well above the national average in Russia and exceeding even the wages of some skilled technicians. His eldest son was studying at the Institute for Northern Peoples in Leningrad, a political education centre from which he would return to the Chukchi land as another proselytiser of the Communist faith. And one evening he, Afanasi himself, as if to proclaim the sophistication he had attained to, switched on his battery radio, and I heard, drifting out of his tent and across the melancholy spaces of the tundra, the familiar, warm, exotic rhythm of the blues, broadcast on the regular evening transmission of the Voice of America. There could be no surer sign of progress than that.

·   ·   ·

Day merged into night and back into day without visible distinction. Only our watches told us the meaningless time. We would breakfast at five in the afternoon and dine at mid-day, or

go to sleep at ten in the morning and rise to an aperitif of cognac
and a light snack of boiled reindeer at three. Our minds and
our bodies succumbed entirely to a life where there was neither
past nor future but only the same insomniac present; our memories
dissolved in a time continuum without landmark or goal. The
sun was hidden perpetually by a blanket of grey cloud from
which issued forth—from time to time—either rain or snow;
the wind from the pole blew unceasingly and froze us to the bone.

We were, without doubt, the first Englishmen to tread these
wilds in half a century. The thought gave us no comfort. Seventy
years before, a certain Lord Clifford had roamed these parts shooting at geese and gluttons, but he left no record of his stay and we
did not seriously seek to emulate him. At certain moments of
what in more southerly latitudes would be called the day or the
night, we set off with Charlie Chan and the two remaining
officials of Nizhnye to pot at wildfowl round a distant lake, but
our heart wasn't in it. John was armed with a twelve-bore and I
carried a .22 and our pockets jingled with ammunition as we
ducked out of the tent and trudged off in the snow to seek our
prey. Probably we were the only armed Englishmen in the entire
Soviet Union at that time, but again the thought brought us no
satisfaction, for we were cold and hungry and the walking was
abominable. The snow that had covered the tundra in a smooth
white blanket when we arrived was melting now, revealing bogs
into which we stumbled, and foot-high tussocks of heaved soil
and sedge over which we fell. The lake was a long way away and
the few geese and duck that had yet ventured up from the south
were all felled by the gleeful, gibbering, abominable Charlie
Chan. He had steadily been working his way through the bottles
of brandy we had been made to pay for, and though they made
him sit down very heavily now and then they never affected his
shooting, which was deadly and left nothing for anybody else
to fire at. When he had disposed of the wildfowl, he threw the
empty brandy bottles up in the air and disposed of them too.
There was no holding him when he had a gun in his hand.

It is so cold in the Siberian tundra that the animals which

are obliged to live there have furry noses and woolly ears. Even the soles of the ptarmigan's feet are covered in feathers, and in the winter the Arctic fox, which is blessed with the ability to endure a temperature of —40° without having to get up and walk around to keep warm, changes the colour of his coat—not, as is popularly thought, to disguise himself against the snow, but so that the pigments in the cells of his fur can be replaced by warm, insulating air. There were times on the tundra when I envied these animals their inherited equipment to defeat the cold that sneaked through the chinks in my inferior, man-made pelt. My teeth chattered even if I lay fully-clothed inside my thick sleeping-bag; not even the brandy could keep me warm.

So those curious tundra days passed; Afanasi's mother brought the saucepan of reindeer meat at intervals; Charlie Chan passed the bottle; sometimes we were allowed a sliver from the salami sausage and sometimes, when the others had lurched off with their guns, John and I were able to get some sleep. It snowed and it rained alternately; once a thick mist descended and very occasionally the sun peeped down at us; all the time it thawed, so that soon the tundra had become a swamp and my felt boots leaked icy water. Reindeer sleighs arrived at Afanasi's camp from time to time, bringing sacks and bundles; occasionally he departed on a sledge, accompanied by his favourite husky dog, to inspect his herd. Life went on.

On the last night of our stay Charlie Chan was in very high spirits. It had been a very enjoyable holiday away from the *Pravda* office in distant Yakutsk. His bag of birds was large by now and included not only geese and duck but teal as well and one snowy owl. He was, moreover, six bottles up on the rest of us.

He came into the tent, laid his gun against the tent wall, pulled off his rubber boots and said, "I know a funny joke."

We glowered at him out of our sleeping bags. "Yes?" we said.

"A Russian came into a Yakut house," Charlie continued, "and looked up at the ceiling. He saw a pair of gloves hanging down from the rafters and he said 'What is that hanging from the ceiling? Tell me.'"

He looked at us expectantly.

"Go on," John growled.

"So the Yakut replied . . . ha ha . . . the Yakut replied, 'A cow's udder.' "

Charlie Chan doubled up with laughter on his camp bed.

"Go on," John said.

"That's it. That's it. Don't you see? A cow's udder!"

I never thought Charlie Chan had much of a sense of humour, but perhaps, after all, I had misjudged him; perhaps here was the palaeolithic fountainhead of all comedy, the first blinding discovery of metaphor that had led down the ages to the minstrel jester and the court fool, Buster Keaton and Laurel and Hardy, the banana skin and the custard pie. I looked at Charlie Chan as he squirmed and shrieked on his bed. Perhaps this was how it was, I thought, when humour made its first stuttering, unfledged flight into the primeval world, among the caribou bones in the firelight at the mouth of the cave. Perhaps that was it.

Encouraged by our lack of response, Charlie spoke again.

"I know another one just as funny," he said. "It's about a —"

"Don't call us," John interrupted, "we'll call you. Let me tell you one of mine. A man goes to see his psychiatrist. 'Doctor,' he says, 'I want you to help me.' 'What seems to be the trouble?' the psychiatrist asks him."

Charlie listened attentively. He took off his fur hat.

" 'Well, you see,' John went on, 'I'm suffering from loss of memory.' 'Aha,' the psychiatrist says, 'and how long has that been going on?' 'How long has what been going on?' "

I laughed. John laughed. Charlie frowned.

"What happened then?" he asked.

"That's it," John said. "That's the joke."

"I don't think," Charlie pontificated solemnly, "one should make mock of mentally ill people."

He shuffled down into his sleeping bag.

"*Dobroy nochi*," he said. "Good night."

When I awoke the next morning I saw Charlie ride over the horizon on a white horse. He looked very splendid and proud on horseback in the wilderness and mentally I made a note to forgive him his boorishness on the previous evening and to ask him where he found the horse.

Not long afterwards the helicopter returned. One could hear it far across the tundra and when it arrived, beating the air above us, it seemed like an unwarranted intrusion on our isolated little lives. We dismantled our tent, stowed our gear, bade our farewells to Afanasi and his wife and mother, and clambered aboard. Like a gnat we rose into the air, turned once above the Chukchi tents and buzzed east towards Nizhnye and the start of the long return journey to Moscow. We could go no further on. We could only go back.

Beneath us was the tundra, leaden and dead. Soon the sun would warm its thin and arid soil, and the lichen wastes would bloom suddenly with saxifrage and yellow Arctic poppy, and the air would be full of butterflies and bees and the cries of southern birds in the hot transient summer. But not yet. And not for us.

10

The Land of the White Death

HE was sitting at the table next to us; though the Lena Restaurant in Yakutsk was crowded, he sat alone. Beer had come into town that day and everyone was making the best of it. The man at the next table had four bottles lined up in front of him together with a carafe of Siberian spirit; he was evidently determined to get drunk.

We had finished our lunch and were waiting for the tea we had ordered when he leant over to us and said, "Come and sit at my table." We made some demur—but he insisted, and there was something about his manner, some desperate authority, that made us join him.

"Have a drink," he said. "Vodka, beer, cognac, Georgian wine—anything you like. Pass your glass. Come on."

He filled our water tumblers with beer.

"Where do you come from?" he asked.

We told him, England.

"I've met many nationalities in my time," he said, "but never English. That's *their* luck!"

We didn't know, at the time, what he meant. It became very evident later.

"As for me," our friend went on, "I'm Russian!"

The vehemence with which he spat this out was startling and very strange. I had met Russians who patently disavowed the State, or even Communism, but I had never before met one who went so far as to disavow his country, his own Russian-ness.

"That is to say I was born in Russia and my mother was Russian. My father, on the other hand, was a Czech. That was probably the biggest mistake he ever made in his life. That was a crime, terrible, unforgivable."

He was a short man but very broad and muscular; his fingers were short, thick and strong and his face carried an air of embittered and mocking defiance, as though he couldn't give a damn and would fight like a cornered animal not to be made to.

"In the famine before the war—before you were born, I expect—my father, my dear, beloved father, fell into a grievous error. Shall I tell you what he did? He gave away his grain stocks—*gave* them away, he didn't sell them. There were old women starving in his village because they had nothing to eat, they were dying all round like flies, so he fed them. He gave away fifteen per cent of his grain altogether. Wasn't that the right thing to do? Don't you think that was a good thing to do, the act of a good man? Don't you?"

"Yes," said John, "it was."

"My father was denounced for what he had done. They pointed to him and said, 'You are an enemy of the people!' That's what they said. They said, 'What you have done is a crime against the State. The corn is the State's and you have disposed of it.' Disposed of it!"

He took a long drink from his glass. His hand was trembling and there was a choke in his voice.

"They hung my father like a common criminal."

He turned away from us and looked out of the window. He was crying.

"After they had executed my father I became head of the family. I was their eldest son. In those days some of us owned a little land and the State didn't like it. They wanted the land. And they took it. And they sent the owners of the land to prison. Well, I was the head of the family and we owned a little land and I was sent to prison. That was a long time ago—and here I am now, on holiday, you might say, in Yakutsk."

He fumbled in his pocket and brought out a heap of paper scraps. He rummaged through the papers until he found what he was looking for and passed it over to us. It was a letter, written

in a large, shaky, female hand, in a Slavonic that John could
not decipher. It was evidently of considerable age, that precious
letter, for it was crumpled into a thousand creases, the pencil
had faded and the paper was greasy and shiny from handling
over a long period. For how long, I wondered, had he been
carrying it in his pocket?

"Go on, read it," he said.

John pretended to read it.

"It's from my mother."

Slowly it dawned on us what this man's fate had been. Where
had he come from that he was forced to spend his holiday in
Yakutsk of all places? He had been sent to prison in Stalin's
time, a kulak and son of a kulak, and the rest of his life he
had spent—where? We hardly needed to guess.

"I haven't seen my mother in years," our friend went on.
"I've spent most of my life out here. I have a son, too, somewhere. He'd be about your age now—young, strong, a future
to look forward to. But I've never seen him. I don't suppose
I ever shall."

He refilled our glasses.

"My friends, I give you a toast—to youth, to the young. You
are young enough to be my sons. I wish you well, Englishmen.
I hope you have better luck."

He was not sad any more; his old embittered defiance had
returned.

"I suffer from angina now. They say there's a cure for it.
But who cares? I don't, and I'm quite sure no one else does."

I was suddenly aware that we were being observed. The restaurant had largely emptied while he was talking and I saw that
the manageress was hovering anxiously in the background,
obviously embarrassed that this man and John and myself should
be talking together, and trying to pluck up courage to intervene.
It was not a good thing, clearly, that we should be seen talking
to a man with a past, an anti-social element, if not a subversive
reactionary.

Our friend stood up. "I'd like you to meet some of the more

cunning moujiks of this town," he said. "Some of our more cringeing comrades." He pointed to the two Russians sitting quietly at a corner table. "Come and meet them, come and talk to two real live peasants!"

"Who are you?" the men demanded angrily.

"Ah, my peasant friends! I would like you to meet two English journalists, acquaintances of mine. *They* at least know red from white."

The men didn't want to meet us.

"Be on your way!" they told him angrily. "You drunken moujik."

It was then that the manageress came up. "I would like a word with you," she said. But he ignored her and turned to us. "Come to my place," he said, "where we can all say what we like."

We followed this unhappy man out of the door. The manageress called out again, a last despairing subterfuge to detach him from our company. "You've left your documents behind on the table," she called, but again he ignored her.

As we passed the hotel entrance I made an excuse to go up to my room to collect some photographs. A few minutes later John followed, "to look for me". Shortly afterwards there was a knock on the door. A maid was standing there. "Is it true that this man, who has a taxi and says you are his guests, is expecting you?" she asked.

John turned to me. "It's more than his life is worth to be seen in our company any more." He turned to the maid. "Yes," he said, "it's true. But we have work to do. Could you ask him if he could excuse us — and tell him we're sorry."

A guilt-ridden gloom descended on us. We had betrayed another man's confidence, treacherously kicked away his friendship. Who else could he have gone to in that bleak and lonely and frightened town? To what other human being in that whole wide world could he offer a drink and show a letter from his aged mother? For his sin had been to suffer but not to forgive, and his exile had never ended.

.   .   .

Peter the Great started it. In 1710 he despatched a small group of undesirables to Siberia; it was cheaper than imprisoning them and they could do useful work while they were there. Succeeding Tsars followed his example. By 1823 a continuous stream of convicted criminals were trudging off to the living death of the Siberian forced labour camp, and within a few years their numbers were augmented by political deportees who had been sentenced to varying periods of exile in the remoter parts of the east. In some years as many as 18,000 persons crossed the Urals into servitude; within fifty years 772,979 prisoners and exiles had been peremptorily disposed of in this way.

Many of these unfortunates were hard-case criminals — murderers, robbers, violent and unlawful men that no society could have tolerated. But a great many others were sent to Siberia for wholly absurd or petty reasons, for taking snuff or tobacco, for prize-fighting, for fortune-telling, for driving a horse by its reins or felling a tree without permission. Siberia was the easy solution to the problems of unwanted minority groups, such as the Poles and the Jews and religious non-conformists, and it was not only the poor and the underprivileged who suffered, for many an aristocrat out of favour with the Court was summarily banished to the wilds from which he was unlikely ever to return. By 1882, when the deportation rules were classified, exile and the slave-camp had become such arbitrary and habitual forms of punishment in Russia that innocent and guilty alike were liable to them; any serf who incurred his landlord's displeasure was immediately despatched; no warrant, no charges and no witnesses were required to banish anyone deemed "prejudicial to public order or incompatible with public tranquillity", and as a result thousands were sent to their death because of some random whim or grudge. Siberia became the ultimate expression and enforcement of the repressive autocracy of the Tsar; it became not only the dumping ground of the scum of Russia but the repository of those intelligent and liberal elements of the population who sought — often in the most harmless way—to limit the power of the Tsar and ameliorate the terrible conditions of the common man in Russia.

Before the completion of the Trans-Siberian Railway the deportees had to walk the thousands of miles to their destination along the great Siberian *tract*, the overland route to Irkutsk. The journey sometimes took as long as four years and often only half of the prisoners survived it. Each prisoner was fettered by leg-irons weighing five pounds; his head was half shaved and a diamond-shaped piece of cloth, listing the crimes for which he was convicted, was stitched to his back. If he was a criminal he was declared legally dead; he lost all civil rights, all paternal rights over his children and all matrimonial rights over his wife; his property passed on to his heirs. In convoys of 300 or 400 persons, through blizzard, rain, mud and dust, lashed by the leather knouts of the guards, sick, hungry, covered in lice, without hope, the prisoners trudged eastwards to the purgatory of the mines and camps of Siberia. In the villages they passed through they sang the terrible *miloserd-naya*, the exiles' begging song. "Have pity on us, O our fathers," they sang, "have pity, O our mothers, have mercy for Christ's sake . . . " And they held out their caps, into which the villagers would drop coins and pieces of bread. "If you can imagine these words," wrote an eye-witness at the end of the nineteenth century, "half sung, half chanted, slowly, in broken time, on a low key, by a hundred voices, to an accompaniment made by the jingling and clashing of chains, you will have a faint idea of the exiles' begging song. It seemed to be the half-articulate expression of all the grief, the misery and the despair that had been felt by generations of human beings on the *étapes*."

Some of those who survived the journey were sent to the notorious gold mines of Kara or the equally grim lead mines at Merchinsk on the Mongolian border; some were assigned to work projects in the far East; others faced another long and terrible march northwards to the Arctic, from which escape was impossible and death the only release. For those who attempted to evade or resist their hopeless and degrading servitude there was the prospect of years of solitary confinement, a diet of bread and water in below-freezing cells, a hundred lashes of the knout and the persecution of the guards who were often as brutalised by the inhumanity of it all as the prisoners themselves. Typhus and scurvy carried off thousands quickly; others succumbed more slowly to exhaustion, malnutrition and moral collapse.

The fate of the non-criminal political exiles was different. They went, not to prison or forced labour camps, but to places of enforced detention in villages, towns or even cities. They could bring their wives and families with them, and their chattels and books. They wore civilian clothes, were able to conduct business or pursue their professions (other than teaching or medicine), and take part in an active social life. Among many of the officials and military of Siberia they were well received and befriended, for they were men and women of intelligence and culture in a largely barbarian land. Before 1905 there was never a great number of them, and during the nineteenth century they represented only three to four per cent of the deportees to Siberia. By the end of that century little more than a hundred of them each year were sent into exile, but they were an inordinately important group. Many of them were specialists in such subjects as law, engineering, science and the arts, and some of the Government officials in Siberia were sufficiently public-minded to make use of these talents, of which the country had dire need. Thus it was due to the exiles that the first official census of Siberia was carried out; they explored and mapped large areas of unknown land; collected material for museums and valuable ethnographical data; wrote monographs and books on Siberian problems and contributed to Russian magazines. The Decembrist exiles of 1825 had founded the important Siberian city of Chita, and it was a community of religious fanatics, called Skoptsi, exiled to Yakutia on account of their unacceptable practice of mutilating and eliminating the sexual organs of both men and women (in order, they thought, to destroy the sources of all sin), who were the first to introduce scientific agriculture into that region and experiment with new seeds and mechanical equipment.

But it was after 1905 that the political exile came into his own in Siberia. After the unsuccessful revolution of that year, 100,000 suspects and sympathisers were rounded up and herded off to the east. Among them were Lenin, Stalin, Trotsky and many others who were later to play a key part in the overthrow of the last of the Tsars of Russia. Suddenly these men were given something they had hitherto lacked. They were given time; time to think, to write, to organise; time to study the classic writings of the scientific Socialists, to learn Marxist theories, revolutionary techniques and the problems of rule. Between duck-hunting and wood-cutting, the future leaders of Russia received their political education, and when the Revolution came in 1917, they put what they had learnt to good effect. The Government was overthrown; a new order and a new deal for the masses was established; the iniquities that had made Siberia what it was were at last, it seemed, at an end and the exile population was reduced to nil.

It is one of the terrible paradoxes of history that what the Revolution had aimed to sweep away in 1917 it very soon resuscitated. It is one of the tragedies of modern Russia that, where the Tsars had failed, the Communists, with unparalleled ruthlessness, succeeded.

The facts are plain. In 1912, 183,949 persons were in prisons and labour camps throughout Russia, the maximum number in the last years of Tsarist rule. Only ten years after the establishment of Soviet rule this number was exceeded. Four years later the total had reached two million. By 1937, only twenty years after the October Revolution, the penal population of Russia was over six million persons. Where the Tsars had condemned the people in the name of the Tsars, the Communists condemned the people in the name of the people—but on a scale the Tsars could never have dreamed of. Thirty years after a revolution had freed a nation from centuries of servitude, some sixteen per cent of the manhood of that nation was enslaved. Siberia was again synonymous with deportation and death.

It had always been the policy of the Tsars to use prison camps to develop the natural resources of Siberia more speedily and more cheaply than could be managed by a free working population. That they failed was due rather to the utter inefficiency of the regime rather than to some flaw in their conception of this policy. When the Soviets came to power they were faced with the same problems, and when they initiated the first Seven-Year Plan in 1927 they turned to the same solution. The grotesque nightmare of the Stalinist labour camps began. Siberia was re-populated.

The mind boggles at the massive injustice of those years. Never before in history had one people been so terrorised and persecuted by their own kind on such a scale; the individual miseries were swallowed up in the collective disaster, and entire communities, entire races even, were decimated. On the slightest pretext, or on no pretext at all, millions were despatched to the eastern outback, to dig for ores, build roads, railways, airfields and harbours, to construct new towns, power houses and dams. A large part of this penal labour force was composed of men who were innocent and loyal to the State. For them, at least, the hopes and the sacrifices of 1917 had been in vain.

I have never come across a more terrible example of the iniquities of this period of Siberian history than in the case of the goldfields of the Kolyma, from whose lower reaches I had just returned. At the beginning of the 1930s north-east Siberia was an almost uninhabited, unexplored land; it was Siberia at its worst—bleak, desolate, inimical to men, without sustenance, roads or towns. Its only claim to attention was the possibility that somewhere in its cheerless interior there might be gold.

Stories of the presence of gold in the Kolyma region were common in the legends of the natives, but there was never any evidence of its existence until, in 1910, a fugitive convict brought out a small bag of gold from a spot near the Upper Kolyma whose whereabouts he refused to divulge. He jealously guarded his secret, and soon after the Revolution, on one of his many prospecting trips, he died.

Then, in 1925, a White officer, Nikolayev, who had taken an active part in the military operations against the Bolsheviks in the Far East during the Civil War, took advantage of the general amnesty in 1922 to emerge after three years in the taiga. He came out with a few ounces of platinum and deposited it in the State Bank in Irkutsk. The platinum itself was not highly valued, but its presence strongly indicated the presence of gold nearby.

Nikolayev, after adopting Soviet citizenship, offered to help with maps, and soon the prospectors went in. But the real turning-point came later in the year. Inconceivable though it sounds, a party of geologists discovered an unknown mountain range 10,000 feet high in parts, stretching almost 1,000 miles from the Upper Kolyma towards the River Yana in a belt 250 miles wide.

This extraordinary discovery changed the whole concept of the mineral wealth of the country. Within a short time it led to the finding of oil, coal, graphite, mica, phosphorites, marble, iron, copper, tin, lead, zinc, wolfram, molybdenum, silver, platinum, precious stones, and, above all, great quantities of gold. The empty quarter, it seemed, was prodigal in its riches.*

Commercial mining of the gold began in 1927 when there were sixty-five prospectors and 108 men living in adjoining settlements. The prospecting for the gold was done on a private enterprise basis and little of it reached Russia. Most of it was sold to the Japanese, who were at that time free to ply the Kolyma shore of the Sea of Okhotsk.

The Revolutionary Government was, naturally, eager to get its hands on the gold, but at first there seemed only two ways, and both of them were impossible; either to allow free-enterprise prospectors, which was ideologically unacceptable; or to pour in Government money, which was out of the question because of the State's crippling financial crisis. There was, however, a third way.

In 1931 a special administration, called DALSTROY, was set up for the purpose of developing north-east Siberia with slave labour. The matter was urgent. Russia's gold reserves had

---

* Earlier Lenin had prophesied: "When we achieve victory on a world scale we will use gold I believe to build public lavatories in the streets of the largest cities of the world."

been seriously depleted; and the country's economy was barely recovering from the successive blows of the Great War, the Revolution and the chaos left by the Intervention. At the same time, millions of peasants in European Russia and the Ukraine were strongly resisting the Government's collectivisation programme, thereby disrupting the agricultural productivity of the nation and blocking one of the State's principal policies. All that was required in these circumstances was a simple equation, and there was no man better qualified to make it than Stalin. He had himself served seven periods of exile in Siberia, on occasion within the Arctic Circle; he knew what it was like, how it could be endured; he had no compunction whatever in sending others to the same fate. If the peasants refused to work on their own land and contribute to the State, they would be made to work elsewhere and contribute in another way. In 1932 the first human cargoes began to arrive at Nagayev Harbour (later renamed Magadan) on the southern coast of Kolyma.

Each steamer that arrived in that year carried 8,000 to 12,000 prisoners in its hold; when they passed Japan on their nine-day journey the hatches were battened down; secrecy was a necessary ingredient of the human tragedy that was to ensue. Not all the slaves reached land safely. In 1933, for example, DALSTROY decided to land prisoners on the north coast of Kolyma, to join up with those who were building a road from the south. In that year the S.S. *Dzhurma*, with 12,000 prisoners on board, set out from Vladivostock bound for the Lower Kolyma. The sailing had been mis-timed, however, and winter found the ship frozen in the sea-ice. For nine months the prison-ship was subject to the horrific weather of a Kolyma winter, and when summer came and the ship landed at Ambarchik, a little down-river from Nizhnye Kresty, all the 12,000 slaves were dead. Half the crew were insane when the ship finally docked in Vladivostock.

Magadan had a fine natural harbour but its hinterland was uninhabited and bare. The slave's first task was to build houses for the guards and technical and administrative staff of DALSTROY. Then piers and harbour installations had to be constructed, and roads up the steep cliffs, and saw-mills, brickyards, a fish-salting factory, repair-yards and a power station. Throughout the summer thousands laboured on building a road from the rising port to the gold fields inland; they worked in the ragged clothes in which they had arrived, standing knee-deep in the swamps under a continuous pouring rain; their food was meagre and the weaker among them soon died off; epidemics broke out and carried off the strong. When the first winter set in no accommodation had been built for the prisoners; blinding blizzards blew for weeks on end over their summer camps, and many of the advance parties in the taiga were cut off from supplies for several months. Of the many thousands who had left Magadan in the summer less than a hundred returned in the spring. Ironically, the road for which they had given up their lives was torn to pieces by the frost and engulfed by mud in the thaw. A stretch one mile long had 80,000 beams laid across it before it finally held.

Between 1932 and 1941 the original labour force of west Russian kulaks was augmented by vast influxes of Latvians, Lithuanians, Poles, Jews and other discredited nationalities, together with the survivors of the Stalinist purges. The port was built, the road was completed, and the gold-mines of the Kolyma valley were put into operation. The Second World War brought captured Germans, Italians, Finns, Hungarians and Japanese, and within a few years Kolyma became the principal gold-bearing region of the USSR. The cost, in terms of capital expenditure, was ridiculously small; in terms of human expenditure it worked out, quite simply, at one man's life for every kilogram of gold that was mined.

There were probably more than fifteen million slaves in forced labour camps throughout Russia at the time of Stalin's death. Gradually they were released to fumble their way back into ordinary life again. Were they all as bitter, I wonder, as our friend in the Lena Restaurant in Yakutsk? Could the comforting slogans in the streets of the cities, the platitudes uttered by Moscow Radio, the beguiling comments in the Party newspapers, the pride and the hopes and the achievements of Communism mean anything to any of them any more, who had spent the prime of their lives behind barbed wire for no cause?

To-day some social parasites are still sentenced by Comrade Courts to exile at construction sites, but the bulk of the work in Siberia is now undertaken by young volunteers, men and women freely recruited on a contract basis from the cities of European Russia and the Ukraine. Three million of them have emigrated to Siberia in the last decade (more than the total number of immigrants in the three centuries between 1600 and 1900) and the population of the new towns and settlements is expanding rapidly. Most of the immigrants are attracted there by the new opportunities and by the freedom from ideological pressures which so marks life in the westerly cities. Above all they are attracted to the pay. You can earn big money in Siberia by ordinary Russian standards. An ordinary seaman in the Far East, for example, can earn as much as a factory manager in Moscow, and I met a communications engineer from Leningrad on a tour in Yakutsk whose pay and allowances amounted to 1,000 roubles a month—nearly five times what he was earning at home. Pay increases with latitude (in the high Arctic it can be as much as 100 per cent more than the national average) and with length of service (a ten per cent increase for every one or two years served). Siberia's name is being cleaned up and an essential part of the process is the obliteration of the past. To-day the building of Magadan is ascribed to teams of Young Communist Volunteers. What else could they say?

11

Idyll in Irkutsk

I HAD been away from Irkutsk for nearly a month and when I came back it had changed almost beyond recognition. I had first arrived there in May, in the cold grey light of a pre-spring dawn. There had been no leaves on the trees then, and no grass growing anywhere; this part of Siberia, even in that late month, seemed numbed and petrified by a winter that had been the longest and cruellest in living memory, and I recall the early-morning street cleaners wrapped in furs and padded quilt jackets, wielding their brooms of birch twigs down streets that had been terribly clawed and gouged by the winter ice.

The ice and snow had gone by the time I arrived and the bone-dry Siberian wind had removed the last vestiges of the thaw, the floodwaters and the sloshing mud. Then the city was as pinched and wan as a patient after a long illness, and a kind of seasonal hush hung over the place, a feeling of brooding and waiting, like the stillness before a summer rainstorm.

It was the same when I drove in the battered Volga out of the city and down the long, broken road that led through the forest. The trees of the forest crowded down to both sides of the road like chilled and ragged old men huddled together with their backs to the bitter wind. Viewed from a distance the evergreen cedars and pines and the leafless silver birches formed a pelt, grey and dark green in patches, resembling the poor, thin fur of a moulting animal after a lean season. The forest at that time depressed me; it looked vast, unwelcoming, dark and full of no good; it stirred, as nowhere else has ever done, the long-buried fantasies of my childhood. As my car shuddered and rattled over the potholes of the forest road I would be overcome by a melancholy so severe that I would lapse into long silences and scarcely notice the mournful expanse of trees that so oppressed me. In those pre-spring days of May the great Siberian taiga seemed to chant an ancient and lugubrious dirge that I could hear but could not understand. So strange was this lament, so distant and unfamiliar to my too-sophisticated city ears, that I could feel nothing more than an unease, as if the long-forgotten dull roots of my being had shivered at the touch of rain. I was glad to turn back and reach the town and find a sort of refuge in the warmth of a noisy crowd of heavily drinking, heartily guzzling Russians and Mongols in the restaurant of the Central-noya Hotel. There at least the forest could not bear down on me.

But the next time I travelled that forbidding road, only two weeks later, everything was quite different.

The day had not had a propitious start, for the previous evening I had made the acquaintance of a lonely gentleman from Tokyo who, conscious of his isolation in the vastnesses of a gigantic continent whose language he could not speak, was as unhappy as a lungfish in a sand desert. He, bowing like a mandarin and trying hard with a manouevring of his fist and manipulation of his lips to hide his very large, protruding, yellow, caricature-Nippon teeth, had been so delighted to find I spoke English that he insisted I share and even drain his treasured bottle of 'Gold Nikka' Japanese whisky, and he had produced this splendid reproduction piece bearing a royal coat of arms surmounted by a stag's antlers and enclosed in a net of gold wire, and with infinite charm and good manners had made me become drunk. "Japanese whisky for doctor colleagues at Budapest," he said, refilling my glass. "But Budapest long, long way." And a demonic laugh struggled for life behind the tombstones of his teeth, was sucked down his throat and died, it seemed, of choking. The bottle was almost finished before an Intourist official appeared at my Japanese friend's side and led him, protesting and bowing violently, to his waiting plane. I was left to grapple with the product of some oriental distillery, the fumes of which lay uneasily upon my system all that night.

So when morning came I did not feel well disposed towards it. The astonishingly liquid and translucent light hurt my now photophobic eyes and the backfirings of the Russian traffic startled me as if I had been suffering from shell-shock. I noted that a brilliant blue sky arched over town and forest but the miracle of this fact escaped my blurred consciousness. I felt that the air was warm but I was not yet sentient enough to feel in it the throbbing of a new vitality, the promise of a remarkable change in the nature of things, of a hot day coming. Only when Nikolai, my Ukrainian driver, rummaging in his tool box, produced the traditional Russian hair of the dog—vodka chased by heavily salted tomatoes—did I shake off my nausea. Then, uncoiling like a dormouse after a long sleep, shuddering to life again at the touch of the bright, warm air, I poked a tentative snout out of my nest, so to speak, and observed with a rare clarity of vision and an immense satisfaction that the winter was gone and summer had arrived. A sudden wind descended on the town and blew the white blossoms from the trees as we drove along the road; the petals filled the air like driven snow so that momentarily the sun was blotted out and the city was covered in a white, perfumed mantle.

Summer in Siberia: the silver birches in leaf now, the whole forest a cheerful and vibrant green; bright wildflowers whose names I could never hope to learn clumped at the roadside, littered like torn-up love-letters in the undergrowth or pushing out of the clay banks, tumescent in the sensuous embrace of the new warm weather. The forest was alive again; the gloom had gone. On the right the Angara river gleamed between the trees like a thin molten lava stream and when the road approached it and ran along it I could see the water in the shallows was as green as the sea over a coral sand-bar; on the other side of the river blue, heavily timbered hills fell steeply to the water's edge. The sun shone from a clear sky and made the earth sing.

Nikolai, holding the steering wheel as if it were a divining rod, smoking a *papirosa* clenched between his teeth, turned to me at length and said, simply and with great feeling, "Oh, ours is a very, very beautiful country!" And on that morning I agreed with him. The crushing, constricting weight that life in the Soviet Union had imposed on me momentarily lifted and I experienced a sense of freedom that was new to me in my stay in that country. Soon the forest thinned a little and opened out on to a big rolling landscape of low, blue-grey ranges of hills against which the receding forest lapped like a sea-tide. I became aware, with a growing feeling of exhilaration, of the hugeness of the Siberian spaces, of an horizon that seemed to circumscribe the sky. It was as if I had woken in a house at which I had arrived after nightfall and had pulled back the curtains of my room to stare in disbelief not at the expected garden but at a vast and primordial landscape upon which the bright morning shone as if it was the first in creation.

The vision quickly faded as the forest closed in again upon the road. We continued in silence, Nikolai deftly avoiding the pot-holes and the fallen-away edges and gently easing the rattling Volga in and out of the switchback sections where the narrow splash of tarmac had subsided when the ground had thawed. We passed occasional villages of newly-painted wooden houses stretched down the length of a single dirt street where women filled buckets from a well and tottered away carrying the buckets on yokes slung along their shoulders; and ponds where children fished with home-made rods; and a cemetery hidden among the trees towards the river, with wooden crosses painted in blue; and a group of white horses, still and statuesque like a Stubbs painting, at the edge of the river which had broadened immensely as it approached its effluent and into which the hills on the further side tumbled as precipitately as the hills of Skye fall into the Sound of Sleat.

It was a very beautiful summer morning; I felt happy and at ease in a world more familiar and sympathetic than Irkutsk or Moscow could ever be. Sitting in the car, watching the trees, the high banks, the river sometimes, the hills and the long fleeting vistas of this immense land pass by me, I remembered other summers no less sudden and joyous, and other places where I had felt, momentarily and incongruously, as equally liberated.

It seemed to me that summer in Siberia was as violent as those desert springs when overnight the sand and gravel plains become pubescent with a shimmer of grass after thirty minutes of rain, and I recalled the one time I had ever seen that phenomenon and how I had felt as exhilarated as I felt now on the forest road beyond Irkutsk. I had been sleeping in the open, I remember, and in the middle of the night I had woken with the soft patter of rain upon my face like the warm fingers of a blind child. Rain in that country after so many hot, windy nights was sensational and in the morning, when I climbed up to the flat rooftop of the mud and coral Arab house where I was living and stared across the plain to the flint mountains, I saw that where once there had been desert there was now an expanse of grass the colour of unripe apples, and that the usually empty sky was full of puffy grey clouds drifting out to sea, and that the wind had veered and that the air was cool and invigorating and that now even the normally enervate Arabs walked the still damp streets with a vigorous, cockerel stride. It pleased me strangely that a little, barely measurable fall of rain could do so much. It always pleases me to see the earth in its old form, to watch the ebb and flow of antique movements across its surface and see life as it was before man gained the power to change and destroy it. Perhaps I have been born out of my time; perhaps at heart I am a cave-man, content with a marrow-bone and a view of a caribou herd, spiritually somewhere back towards the beginning of that troubled road that has led to the present and to the confused vision of life that the Soviet Union has erected round itself like a stockade. But I am glad, nevertheless, to have heard the lions roaring from the kopjes at nightfall and the wild zebras stampeding past my camp at first light; to have watched apples ripen and ragged children laugh and women put up their long hair; seen frozen rivers crack and splinter like glass, trees bow in a wind, corn ripple; drunk mares' milk in a tea-house over a mountain stream, cooked beans in a tin on a wood fire; heard, after an air crash, the chatter of crickets that confirmed I was alive and felt the comforting warmth of the earth; seen a basking shark basking, dolphins leaping, girls dancing and, once, high in the blue sky, a wild white swan which someone shot at and missed. I am grateful to have seen the earth plain, with all its divers forms of living things, and done what men have always thought it good to do. I am glad I could drive through the Siberian forest in the first flush of that brief, quickly-blossoming, quickly-blighted summer. Siberia in that part on that day was a good place to be.

The road bore us along the river bank until, at noon, the view expanded to reveal the shining waters of the great lake beyond which, many miles away, rose a range of snow-capped mountains. We had arrived.

Lake Baikal is not only the deepest lake in the world; it is also one of the coldest. At the eastern end, though we could not see them, seals in white coats still flopped among the ice floes left over from winter; and though the sun still shone brightly from a blue sky, where we were the cold surface of this immense volume of water chilled us and the wind blew strongly now that we were away from the shelter of the trees. Yuri, an ex-Red Army officer who had retired to join Irkutsk Television service, broke some private vow of silence and turned to us and said, "I'm hungry. Let's catch some fish for our lunch. You've tasted *Kharios*, Baikal trout? You like it? It's famous. In Moscow it's a delicacy. Let's catch some and cook it for lunch."

Nikolai, the driver, said, "It's cold out there. The English-men will catch cold."

"Then we'll borrow some coats," Yuri said.

"And some vodka . . ."

"And lines, and hooks and bread . . . why not?"

Already the summer, some call from the forest, had infected us. Already, without knowing it then, we were sliding back through the years to our boyhoods. Were they so very different, those English and Russian arcadian days of many summers past, when the sun shone strongly and time meant nothing beyond a yelp from the belly at noon? We tumbled out of the car and ran down a path, kicking stones and shovelling dust with our insteps, till we came to a group of weather-tanned fishermen by their canoes. With them everything was quickly arranged.

We spent that afternoon fishing on Lake Baikal from a canoe with an outboard motor. Dressed in faded blue, padded winter jackets, free at last from the dreary round of *kolkhoz* and *kombinat*, from the wearisome recital of statistics and record production figures and ideological argument, feeling relaxed in a world of sky and water in the pleasant company of men who were not Heroes of the Soviet Union and never hoped to be, we contentedly pulled fish out of the lake, only occasionally conscious that we were doing so 5,000 miles from home in the heart of a politically estranged land. We had become resigned to such incongruities.

When we had caught enough fish we returned to the bank and built a large fire of dead, dry timber inside the forest. The fisherman who was with us gutted the fish and spitted them on sharpened branches, sticking the branches in the ground in order to grill the fish. We drank vodka round the fire while the fish sizzled and in a little while, after the spirit had started to circulate round our systems, we began to laugh. The clearing in the forest where we sat had become an enchanted glade, a dark green pool into which a grey evening light leaked through the cedar boughs and where bright flowers swam before our vodka-mesmerised eyes like tropical fish. We chortled with unaccountable happiness and I thought, "Haven't I played this game before, in the woods of my childhood, swigging ginger pop and munching green apples in a den in the undergrowth?" The fisherman pulled the cooked fish away from the fire and we divided the portions, throwing them from hand to hand like hot potatoes till they were cool enough to eat. And when we had eaten them and the vodka was finished we got up and wandered around.

We wandered down to the edge of the forest, where the road was and where the flowers grew thickest and there was an elevated view for many miles across the thickly-timbered hills. I busied myself taking photographs. A man in felt knee-boots came down the road leading two cows—"Good day," he said, and I said,

"Good day." And in a little while a small girl came running round the bend and down the hill, running in bare feet with her frock flying and her hair tumbling across her face. When she came up to me and saw me with my camera she called out to me—I couldn't understand what she said but it was plainly unflattering —and as she passed me she turned without stopping and continued running backwards on her toes, holding out her hands to steady herself. As she ran in this way, poised like a ballerina *en pointe*, she called out again, impishly, and made gestures she calculated would spoil my photograph, exaggerating the gestures as the distance between us increased until one final grandiloquent flurry of arms proved too much for her precarious balance and she fell, black knickers in the air, blonde hair in the dirt. "Serves you right!" I shouted in English and she picked herself up and laughed and ran *dump-dump-dump* on her bare feet round the far bend until she was absorbed once again by the silent forest from which she had come.

Suddenly I was filled with nostalgia for my childhood. The little girls of those ancient woods are thirty now and, like me, they have forgotten the smell of the earth, the feel of different grasses, the depth of the sky; I wished that I was a little boy again, and could scrump the orchards, pee down from the tops of trees and chase wild little girls barefoot through the brushwood. I turned towards the others . . .

I suppose because of my work as a photographer I have learnt to see as a camera sees, instantly to release a mental shutter and record in my brain a scene where all motion is frozen at the critical and significant moment; much of my memory consists of a file of such photographs, the action arrested in the lobes of my brain with all the kinetic stillness of figures on a Grecian frieze. So when I turned to my companions and saw what they were doing my shutter clicked, so to speak, and I find I can now reproduce their dispositions within that scene as exactly as if I were examining an image imprinted on silver bromide. The scene in retrospect is pleasantly absurd and perhaps I found it so at the time, for why else should I have fixed it so vividly in my memory?

But at the time, too, it struck me as extraordinarily in harmony with my own mood and as a logical outcome of that strange, idyllic afternoon.

I first saw John. He was wearing Italian shoes, a blazer with Royal Navy buttons, and his Oxford college tie. At the moment I saw him he was hanging at arms' length from the lower branches of a solitary silver birch tree growing on a bluff of red earth above and away from the road; his left leg was bent upwards as if to find a foothold on the trunk of the tree, but his right leg hung straight down like a dead man's; though his back was towards me there was about his attitude a fierce, totally absorbed concentration that was wholly characteristic of him. I had not seen my friend dangling from a tree before, not in Siberia, or anywhere else, but when I saw Yuri I knew that the *cafard*, the spring fever, had not overtaken John alone.

Yuri was wearing a typically Russian grey raincoat and a typically Russian trilby hat—the walking-out uniform of any Soviet bureaucrat. On the lapel of his raincoat was pinned the triangular blue badge denoting that the wearer had received higher education—in fact Yuri had only recently left the Educational Corps of the Red Army to take up an appointment as Press Officer at the local television station. He was short, wore glasses and had the face of a born clown—a large, highly mobile mouth and wide, round eyes that really made mock while appearing to be solemnly attentive; the eyes of a non-conformist hiding behind an overtly conformist aspect, who could always resort to buffoonery as a last resort if ever his disguise was discovered. Yuri was on the other side of the road and he must have spent the last few minutes busily rummaging along the roadside, for at his feet there was now a large pile of stones, each the size of a fist. As I saw him in that split-second of arrested time his squat macintoshed form was leaning backwards, with his left leg braced forwards and his right arm stretched stiffly back. In his right hand he clutched a stone which he was about to propel with great vigour, as if it was a hand-grenade, towards the trunk of a birch tree some fifteen yards in front of him. It occurred to me oddly that no one who had ever played cricket would throw stones at a tree in such a clumsy way —but Yuri was late of the Red Army, so how could he be expected to know? The stone landed with a satisfying clonk against the trunk and Yuri quickly stooped down to gather another one. He threw stones at trees as he played chess—swiftly, seemingly haphazardly, but to dire effect.

Nikolai, too, I transfixed with my beady camera eye during that brief and wholly absurd moment in the Siberian forest. Nikolai was a giant Ukrainian, a bear of a man with a gentle, pock-marked face and hands like enormous raw hams; when he spoke—which was seldom but always to the point—the words fell out like coals shaken through a sieve, rough but promising comfort. Always during the short time I knew him he wore high Russian felt boots, baggy cavalry-style trousers, a thick blue serge lumber-jacket and a cloth cap to match. During the war he had fought on the eastern front and had been a member of one of the first Russian units to enter Berlin; he hated war, loathed all Germans and was immensely proud of his country without ever saying as much. That afternoon he was very content, moving slowly among the bushes and between the trees at the edge of the forest gathering wild flowers to take home to his family; as he emerged, disappeared and re-emerged in the thickets he reminded me of some great, shy wild animal waiting in the African bush for night to fall before venturing to the water-hole, in the meantime gently and warily moving about, feeding—on lilies. He held out his fist as if he was carrying a ceremonial sword, and slowly throttling in that massive paw was a bunch of very beautiful wildflowers—I wish I knew the names of them (how strange and necessary this human urge to label everything, as if by doing so we can make the object immutable and stave off change and decay, the enemies of the orderly mind); but their shapes and now even their colours elude me and though I have just looked at a sample I pressed and sent home, their colours have faded, leaving me with only my erratic memory of them that curious summer a year ago.

I called out to John and my voice shattered the stillness; the petrified figures in my mind's eye jolted to life again, stepped down from the frieze on the broken urn. John fell from his tree like a ripe plum; Yuri heaved his last stone and then abandoned his target; Nikolai lumbered out from the trees clutching his garland and joined us by the car. The spell was broken, the interlude was over, and we drove back through the forest towards the city and the world of the party slogans, the exhortatory banners, the phoney statistics, the symbolic jungle of electricity wires and the long wait for beer and borshch. The scent of the forest was left behind us.

At length Yuri turned to us and said, "Of course, to-day was a holiday. All workers need holidays. Even journalists must have a break, mustn't they? But to-morrow we will go and look at some of the realities of the Soviet achievement in Irkutsk. I have arranged for us to visit the Centre of Higher Education and the new hydro-electric station. It is a very fine new station with an output of 660,000 kilowatts. And after that . . ."

Had I, I wondered, just seen him playing games in the forest and eating fish by an open wood fire? Was it possible that he could conceive of only one kind of reality?

"Journalism is one of the most important professions," he was saying. "In the Soviet Union a journalist is a very important person. He keeps people throughout the State informed of the latest technological progress, and that is very important. In the West your newspapers are full of sexual scandals, murders and bank robberies and the financial exploitations of rich capitalists. Here we prefer to write about real achievements. As journalists we are more aware of our responsibilities to the people."

"But you repress as many facts as you put in," I said. "You print only what your Government wants you to read. Do you consider that being responsible?"

"Of course," Yuri said, "we have our scandals, too. Would we be human without them? But why should we write about dirt? What value is there in that? What amazes us about your newspapers is that you print anything. Take your Christine Keeler, for example. She is a scandal throughout the world. But who is telling the world about her? Not us—you are! We know very well that one or other of our Ministers could get tied up with a girl of easy virtue. But do you think we'd tell everybody about it? Do you think we would get rid of a clever leader because of a slut? After all—a man is a man—he may lose his head at times. But why should we bring our Government into disrepute because of that? Our journalists are not hooligans."

"*Da, da*," we said, "*da, da*."

"It's the same with our writers and artists. They do not want to honour filth, the baser side of life. They want to celebrate the glories of Man's struggle."

"What English writers do you read in Russia?" I asked.

"Dickens is very popular."

"He is in England, too, but for different reasons."

"And Galsworthy. *The Forsyte Saga*. And among modern writers in English we like Steinbeck and Faulkner and Hemingway. And John Braine—*Room at the Top*—and Alan Sillitoe."

"What novels of Hemingway do you read?"

"*The Old Man and the Sea*."

"Any others?"

Yuri thought for a moment. "I don't remember any others. Has he written any others?"

"None that you would like very much," I said. "What did you like about *The Old Man and the Sea*?"

"It gave a very good picture of the economic oppression and social injustice in Cuba before Castro's revolution. It was a shocking picture of poverty—very well written. He was a very gifted writer."

"Yes," I agreed, "it was very well done. It was a very moving story. But I thought it was about the triumph of Man's courage. Didn't Hemingway write 'Man can be destroyed but never defeated'? I thought the book was about an individual fisherman's spirit triumphing in the face of hardship and defeat. I didn't think it was an indictment of the pre-revolutionary fishing industry in Cuba. But it doesn't matter."

We were approaching Irkutsk. We could see the dam across the Angara and the electricity cables looping away into the

Siberian outback with their promise of power and prosperity.
We passed the barrack-like dormitory blocks for the students of
the Higher Education Centre.

"You see," Yuri said, waving his hand towards the window,
"a writer must not shun social criticism where it is due —so long
as he is fair. We are not perfect but we try to be better, work
harder, contribute more. That dam you saw —it has harnessed the
wild river, it provides power for industry, a better standard of
living for our people. That is what we build our faith on —on
progress, on the future. A writer, you must understand, should
write about what Man might be, not about what he is."

The complaining Volga drew up at last by the Centralnoya and
stopped with a sigh. We got out in the pale evening light.

If ever I write again, I thought, I shall write about what Man
is and not about what I am told he might be or ought to be.
If ever I write about this journey through the Soviet Union I
shall write about what the Soviet Union is as I see it and not
about what it might be or ought to be. Being of a very different
and older tradition.

.   .   .

Before we left Irkutsk we attended an ordination service in
Znamyenski Cathedral, one of the three active churches in
Irkutsk. It had three priests and two deacons to serve it; one of
the other churches also had three priests, but in the third church
one priest had died, one priest had retired and another was very
old. The new priest whom we saw ordained that morning was
taking over the under-staffed church. He was twenty-five years
old and had been trained at the famous seminary at Zagorsk,
outside Moscow —a four-year course during which he was
"supported by believers".

The ordination of a new priest into the Russian Orthodox
Church is an event of great rarity in Communist Russia and
permission for us to take photographs of it had to come from the
Patriarch himself. At first he refused (I don't blame him) but
some kind of pressure must have been put on him, for some days
later permission was granted —presumably the Soviet authorities

wished to avail themselves of this opportunity to prove to the world that there was no persecution of Christians and that the churches still functioned freely. This is true, of course, the churches that exist do function, but there are few of them left and they are mostly attended by old women; the priests that serve them, for their own well-being, seldom leave the precincts.*

Znamyenski Cathedral was founded in 1757 and I was told that it had functioned ever since. Since the priest who told me this was in the presence of a Government official there was little else he could say. Until 1924 the cathedral had been a nunnery. In 1956 it was "renovated". Was there perhaps a hint that between these dates the cathedral had not been used? At any rate, that Sunday morning the cathedral was full to the door. It was like that on every feast day, I was told—"The priest drinks whatever wine is left over from Mass and he has never been ill from having too much."

It was a long, very moving service. In spite of everything they had kept their faith, the old people and the priests. The faces of the old women, bound in scarves and shawls, were deeply etched, deeply sad. They prostrated themselves, kissed in turn the paintings of the saints on the walls and pillars, lit candles continually and wept. One of them collapsed on the steps leading to the altar. What lives had these old people led, I wondered, since they had been born? Was I being fanciful to suppose that I saw stamped on their upturned yearning faces the scars of all Russia's history in this century? And what kind of life had Veniamin, the Archbishop of Siberia, led, who now in his white robes and golden crown crossed and lowered the candles he held in bene-diction to the congregation, a small gentle-looking man standing there amid the incense and the beautiful hymns, the ikons and the votaries of his restored cathedral? The service lasted four hours and at the end a collection box was handed round. John put a

* In Moscow there is only one church to every 100,000 of the population, and the great cathedrals of Novgorod, Leningrad, Moscow, Kiev and Riga stand idle or are used as anti-Christian museums. But for some Russians the décor and liturgy of the church still provide beauty and emotion they find lacking in ordinary Communist life, and perhaps for this reason the church still survives.

five-rouble note in it and afterwards, outside in the peaceful green quadrangle, full of trees and flowers and pigeons feeding on crumbs an old lady threw to them, the old women of the congregation clutched our hands and wept.

. . .

The mid-day jet to Moscow naturally took off at three p.m. On board was a large crowd of smart young intellectuals from Peking, and a group of Vietnamese reading Communist political journals of an advanced sort written in French. I wondered where they got their Alitalia, BOAC, Pan Am and Arab Airlines airbags from, but I didn't ask them.

We flew for hours above mushrooming white clouds like the products of some nuclear Armageddon, and when we at last came down there was Omsk again, the identical rectangular blocks of flats rising like dominoes above the wooden houses whose little plots of garden gave the city the appearance of an enormous vegetable allotment. Omsk was hot, scorching with a dry furnace heat that reminded me of Khartoum in the summer. The tarmac was melting and the queues of jostling, straw-hatted Siberians snaked into the ice-cream kiosks. A hot wind gusted over the city, and in the plane the Chinese fans fluttered like a cave full of bats. We were unaccountably grounded for an extra hour and when we did take off it was into the teeth of a dust storm that had already blotted out Omsk in a sandy yellow fog. The dust swept over the flatlands like a polar blizzard and the plane rose from the runway with a crab-like, sideways motion, yawing and sinking in an alarming manner, while the noise of the wind and of the sand scratching the outside skin of the fuselage almost drowned the roar of the engines.

High in the sky the aircraft skirted round the base of a cumulo-nimbus cloud as motionless and permanent-seeming as a mountain. It towered over us, this heap of electricity and turbulence, and we steered round it like a ship avoiding an iceberg. Then came the abyss, the drop to earth and vertigo, and looking back I saw a Great Barrier Reef of overhanging cloud, a permanent back-lit cauldron surmounted at a height of 40,000 feet by an arc of silver cloud, planted like a cross on the summit, Far below, rivers and tributaries lay across the land like the veins of rotted leaves, fingerprints implanted in the soft earth.

We landed at Moscow at seven. It had rained unceasingly for three days and the air was chill and damp. There was no one to meet us and we both felt very tired.

12

The Birthday Party

OUR return to Moscow did not mark the end of our expedition but only an intermediate stage in it. But somehow our sojourn in the depths of Siberia had exhausted us, taken the edge off our enthusiasm; we slept very heavily now, and walked through the streets of the city with a noticeably slower and more reluctant gait. The prospect of a long journey through Central Asia and the southern republics in the height of summer (which was our next intention) filled us with a certain dismay, for I do not think the human body can indefinitely withstand the stress of constant transplanting, nor can the brain endlessly digest a surfeit of new images and all the battering of facts and opinions such an expedition entails. It was clear, too, that after nearly three months in this curiously alien world we were becoming homesick; we were homesick for gaiety and friendship and for all the unimportant little baubles and trifles of life that were so conspicuously lacking there.

Neverthless, during the days we had to wait for our visas and permits for the south to come through, we worked at the various newsworthy events that cropped up. When Tereshkova and Bykovsky came back from outer space we were in Red Square to photograph their triumphal return there; and when they gave a monumental Press conference in Lenin University we were there, too. We attended the World Congress of Women in the Kremlin Palace of Congress the day the Chinese delegation nearly provoked a riot, and we watched in astonishment as they stormed the rostrum, snatched the microphone and attempted to harangue the assembly. "We have the right to be heard!" one of them managed to say. "It is very painful to see such a situation in Moscow." A British delegate who was presiding rang her Chairman's bell and when the tiny, slit-skirted Chinese refused to leave the rostrum, pandemonium broke out. A great crowd converged on the stage. A Frenchwoman cried out, "Here is the Imperialist Press and after that you come to tell us you are against Imperialism!" but no one paid any attention and shortly the Praesidium members began to file from the stage. It was twenty minutes before order was restored, but the 1,000 delegates from 119 countries had been given intriguing food for thought.

There was always something happening in Moscow but there were many empty days also and the maniac summer restlessness that infected the people of the city would infect us too. On such days we would wander down the hot streets beneath the shade of the dusty plane trees and walk along the river or in Gorki Park. We were consumed with a growing sense of isolation and a growing impatience to be off. To stand still in Moscow was to rot a little.

Before we left for the south, however, an unexpected event occurred which I recall vividly and with a certain fondness. It was a Sunday and John and I had spent the day in the country beyond the suburbs. We caught an electric train back to town and at the terminus we boarded a bus to Valkonka, or so we thought. It was only after forty-five minutes that we realised we were going a long way in the wrong direction and when the bus shuddered to a final halt it was clear we were far out on the very edge of Moscow in a seemingly uninhabited suburb of great new apartment blocks. We had arrived at Valkhonka, not Valkonka, a subtle but important distinction that had eluded us. It had rained then, a prolonged, torrential downpour, so that when we did eventually reach our hotel the evening was well advanced and our shoes were soggy and our temper a little frayed. We had barely entered our room when the telephone rang. It was Vadim.

"Hi, you fellers! Where the hell you been? I've been calling you all day. Now listen."

It was his thirty-first birthday. He had arranged a little party in his apartment and he wanted us to join him.

"Come as soon as you can, boys," he said. "My wife's got the dinner on and the drinks are going down like nobody's business."

It was the first formal invitation we had ever received to a Russian home. We felt strangely honoured and happy. We had long become resigned to the Soviet neurosis about foreigners that kept us securely on the outside of the Russian family's front door. Now Vadim's exception to this custom made us sharply aware of it again. It was a custom, I felt, which provoked pity rather than irritation; not all the propaganda in the world could undo the damage this state of fear caused to the Soviet image; I was glad that I lived in a society where it was not necessary.

We caught a taxi to Vadim's apartment block. He was waiting on the street corner to meet us and led us into the building and up a concrete staircase to his flat. Strictly speaking it was not his flat alone, for he had to share it with two other families. But to-day they were away; he could entertain his friends with uncommon expansivenesss.

All the other guests were Russian. They had been there for some time and were happily imbibing a mixture of vodka and American canned orange juice when we arrived. The gramophone was playing a modern jazz composition of Dave Brubeck; strewn around were other American records in glossy folders, and back numbers of *Time* magazine and *Life*. When the Brubeck had finished Vadim put a folk group called The Weavers on the turntable and their sweet harmonies filled the room. "Oh kisses sweeter than wine . . ." Most of the people there were journalists, one or two were connected with the Russian Foreign Service; they had all travelled widely in the world and inevitably they saw no reason why they should not continue to enjoy in Moscow the things they had enjoyed while they were abroad. Someone put on a Frank Sinatra recording: "Only the lonely . . ." We sat around Vadim's little, simple room fingering our glasses and listening to this secreted song from the world beyond, and I thought, "This is the way it ought to be. This is the way it will be."

Our arrival in the midst of these pleasant people momentarily dampened the party. A mood of evasive unease prevailed until we left the sitting-room and went into the dining-room to eat the dinner which Vadim's wife had so carefully prepared. It was another small room, filled mainly by a piano and a large dining table. On this table there was a lavish spread. It was evidently going to be a good meal, and the party warmed again.

When the wine was poured the party warmed even more. Vadim was in an excellent roistering mood and never allowed our glasses or our plates to be empty for long. Russian hospitality, when it had the chance, was boundless.

I do not remember a great deal of that splendid meal, only that it was undoubtedly one of the pleasantest I had ever experienced in the Soviet Union. The steaks were succulent, the side dishes were appropriate, the fruit was varied and fresh, the coffee was first-class, and when the wine was at last finished the cognac came. By the end, late in the evening, the little gathering in that candle-lit room was relaxed and mellow and it had long been forgotten that we were Westerners; we were swept up in the changing moods of the company and passed from polite chatter to boisterous levity and on to a highly-charged, romantic melancholy. During dinner Vadim had led us in many toasts, mostly "to women" or "to love" or variations on those themes; at first these toasts had provoked a measure of joviality, a bantering familiarity which had drawn us closer together, but later—under the influence of the wine and the cognac, the evening drawing in beyond the window and the candles flickering on the table—the mood had changed to a quiet, sad, strange yearning. Vadim's wife left the table then and, taking the candlesticks with her, seated herself at the piano; we waited in silence and shortly she began to play. It was not the music I had expected, for it was not of this time or place; it was Russian certainly, but it was of a very different Russia from that which we could see in the street outside; it was not the traditional folk music of the peasant earth, nor the striding, strident, triumphantly optimistic music of the Soviet faith; it was the still, sensitive music of a different society in a different age, a society whose grace and delicacy had been destroyed in the Revolution of 1917. Suddenly I realised that the curious mood of yearning which descended on the room was being given a positive expression; as the gentle notes of the piano filled the room like a scent of roses, each one of us around that dining table was being transported away from our present circumstances into a world of the imagination where our desires and needs could be met; for our Russian friends this was one of the few means of escape from the harsh realities of Soviet life open to them and it was strange that they chose to escape to the discredited genteel world of the previous century, a world of sensibilities which were no longer recognised in proletarian Russia.

When the piano stopped we shook to life again. A sad, round-eyed, olive-skinned Georgian girl sitting opposite me, who had spent seven years in Paris with her diplomat husband, broke the ensuing silence. Turning those large watery brown eyes upon John and myself, she began to recite, in French, a poem which I dimly knew was by Baudelaire, a poet proscribed in the Soviet Union.

> "*Mon enfant, ma soeur,*
> *Songe à la douceur*
> *D'aller là-bas vivre ensemble!*"

Her voice trembled quietly in the stillness. Was it remembered passion, an intense longing for that never-to-be-regained city that moved her so? Her eyelids closed, hiding the liquid eyes.

> "*Aimer à loisir,*
> *Aimer et mourir*
> *Au pays qui te ressemble!*"

"Oh," she said simply, "Oh." And she paused for a moment, and sighed—for what, for whom? Suddenly the Russian soul, this romantic, manic-depressive thing, was bared to me in that room; I felt for a moment that they too, these Russians I had never met before, were in exile like me.

The men stared into their wine glasses, the white cuffs of their shirts like manacles against the dark table-top and the black cloth of their suits. Vadim's wife was bowed over the piano keys and a slender, svelte young woman on my right, like a residue of the aristocracy, stared mistily into a dim corner of the room. Even the boisterous Vadim was silent.

> *"Mon âme par toi guérie,*
> *Par toi, lumière et couleur!*
> *Explosion de chaleur*
> *Dans ma noire Sibérie!*

The Georgian girl had barely finished when the svelte one woke from her private communion and, throwing her head back, began to sing the theme song from the American film, *The Alamo*. "God!" I heard John say, "what a clash of cultures!" The intense longing that filled these people seemed now too much for us; the words of the film song, sung in this way in this little apartment in the middle of Moscow, were being given an unbearable significance I had not appreciated before. Vadim, conscious that his birthday party was sliding ever more steeply into a trough of melancholy, left the table and went to switch on the gramophone in the next room. Presently even more exotic music boomed forth. It was the Twist.

It was very late when we left. The last memory of that strangely haunting evening was of Vadim, his shirt unbuttoned and his sleeves rolled up, gyrating madly to the music of the Twist. The movements he performed were exuberant but grotesque, for he had little precise knowledge of how this dance should be done and he shook and shuddered his body and limbs in a weird travesty of free expression. When we left he teetered down the staircase as if on rubber springs—each step down a continual surprise to each foot. He told us that soon he was going to England with a Soviet delegation but before that he and his wife were going on a holiday up the Moscow river in a bottle. We asked him if he was sure that he could manage it with two of them in one bottle and he said yes, it was quite a big bottle and he often went out in it with his wife at week-ends. We asked him if many Russians owned bottles and he said yes, in fact there were now several bottle clubs and bottling was becoming quite a popular sport in the Soviet Union. You could bottle up the river for days on end, it was very agreeable.

It was almost the last time we saw him, but on the day before our departure to the south he came to our hotel room, looking a little distressed, and produced a letter from his pocket.

"This letter was addressed to you in Siberia," he told us, "and it was forwarded to our office. I thought I'd open it, in case it was anything important. I'll read it to you. 'Dear Mr Botting and Mr Bayliss. Thank you for your communication from Siberia. The information you sent us was of great interest to us and though we will not make immediate use of it we will keep it on our files for future reference. Please do not hesitate to send us any further information you may obtain.' This letter appears to come from a newspaper in England."

Vadim looked at us quizzically. He was obviously very suspicious.

"What does this mean?" he asked. "What information have you been sending to England?"

"It was about the cuckoo," we explained.

"What is this, the cuckoo?"

"It is a small bird that goes away in the winter and comes back in the spring. When it comes back it goes 'CUCKOO!' That's why it's called a cuckoo."

"But why?" Vadim pressed us, his suspicions not allayed.

"I don't know," John said. "Perhaps it's trying to attract a mate."

"No, no. Why did you send information about this small bird?"

It dawned upon us that perhaps Vadim thought cuckoo was some secret code-word.

"In England it is the custom for some people to write a letter to *The Times* newspaper when they first hear the cuckoo in spring. That's what we did. It was a joke, really. It was a joke to write about it from the middle of Siberia."

Vadim thought for a moment.

"What's funny about the middle of Siberia?" he asked.

"Nothing," we said, "except that it's funny to write about such a thing all the way from Siberia. People only write about it in England."

"What people? What people distribute this information?"

"Oh, retired army officers, landowners, aristocrats, reactionaries, revisionists, a millionaire or two, the odd playboy and ballistic missile station commander. Come off it, Vadim."

"Come off what? Why did you have to join such people? Why did you do it? I wish you hadn't."

But before we shook hands for ever Vadim had forgiven us for our little mockery. He was sad to see us go but we have never heard from him since. He was a good man. We liked him a lot.

13

Deep South Whistle Stop

WE left for Central Asia the next day and flew to Tashkent, the principal city of Uzbekistan. This was the beginning of a long journey through the southern republics of the USSR which was to take us through Samarkand to the Caspian Sea, Armenia and Georgia.

In retrospect it is apparent that we were beginning to suffer from what might be called a congestion of sensory data leading ultimately to constipation of the brain. Certainly my recollection of those weeks is confused; there is no clear pattern of events, other than a remorseless pressing on; but a few cameos—some chance encounters, a landscape, a mood, a phrase remembered—remain clearly etched in my memory. In recalling them I again resort to the journal I kept at the time.

Tashkent was hot, Samarkand was disappointing. The authorities had prevented us from reaching Bukhara so we turned instead to Fergana, "The Pearl of Uzbekistan", a rich oasis in the dusty steppes to which only one Westerner had gone before us in recent years—a French military attaché.

Fergana. July 19. Breakfast at eight in a cool basement café off the main street, while through the shutters one can perceive the day warming up nicely to a crackling heat. I have always loved this hour of the morning in hot countries—in Africa, in Arabia, in Southern Europe. Perhaps it is like coming near to death, one appreciates life much more afterwards: perhaps that is the point in common between the lotus-eater and the adventurer, those two halves of me which constantly pull in opposite directions.

The assistant editor of the local newspaper, an immensely likeable man called Hamdam, has been put in charge of us. After breakfast he takes us to a silk factory, which we do not enjoy, and on to a collective fruit farm, which we do. Here, buried deep in the midst of a vast orchard of peach trees and grape vines, we come upon a pleasant ornamental pool shaded by tall eucalyptus; on the other side of the pool there is an oriental pavilion, and in front of the pavilion is a long banqueting table piled high with bottles and platters of food. "We'll have lunch here, I think," says Hamdam mopping his brow. How he must love looking after special visitors—it was perfectly obvious that this lunch had been laid on for our benefit and had taken the whole morning to prepare.

Lunch was one of the most remarkable meals I have ever eaten. It started at 1.30 and ended eight hours later as night was falling. We started with a toast in vodka, followed this with huge slices of dripping melon dipped into bowls of honey, and continued with soup and pilaff, a stew of meat and various vegetables, innumerable side dishes, hot Uzbek bread, wine, grapes, peaches, pears, bowls of inexhaustible green tea and more vodka. We moved the table to keep in the shade as the sun edged round the glade and the sparrows—those diminutive vultures—pecked at the spot we had vacated. Hamdam, stripped to his yellow vest, talked incessantly, mostly in Uzbek: he was a wag and the two locals who ate with us laughed till it hurt: John and I ate and drank quietly and in perfect contentment.

Fergana. July 20. Away to the mountains at eight. On the borders of Kirghiztan, Hamdam stops the car and says he has brought a bottle of vodka. Behind a kiosk in the border village he drinks from the bottle and chases the vodka with pimentoes and tomatoes which he carefully slices with a penknife. We decline to join him at such an hour.

The hillsides of the lower ranges of the Pamirs are grey and flinty and grass sprouts from the rocky soil like the onset of puberty. Many streams of rushing, soapy-looking water flow down the valleys: in the villages they have placed wooden tea-drinking platforms (called *chaikanas*) over the streams and one sits on a rug in the shade of the trees and listens to the burbling water and is cooled by it in the heat of the day. It is pleasant, this slow, indulgent, curiously graceful life of Asia: a world of donkeys and the occasional horse, of women and girls in red tunics and baggy trousers and round caps selling fruit by the wayside or squatting under trees, and old men, bearded like Genghiz Khan, riding by, like Christ on an ass. The outward manifestations of rural life have changed little over the years: the houses are still mostly one-storeyed rectangular buildings of dried mud, with mud walls enclosing gardens full of trees and shade: one still drinks mares' milk when one halts for refreshment at a roadside inn.

We stop high up in the mountains as it begins to rain and take shelter in a pavilion without walls where the wind whistles through and chills us. A few feet from us a young woman slices onions for the family meal, squatting in a position that would have been inconceivable if she had not been accustomed to it from infancy. The flexibility of her limbs, John remarked, might be taken as an indication of a good performance. Reverie in the wind and the rain: the Anglo-Saxons produced a few concepts and words for love, but they could never have produced the *Kama Sutra*.

Downstairs a lunch of pilaff is prepared for us. Upstairs Hamdam talks constantly and proffers more vodka. He has crushed tomatoes and pimentoes together to produce a juice with which he chases the spirit. I think he was probably grateful to talk to us, for there ran through him a renegade individualism. "I do what pleases me," he said, "and what I think is right. I get told off for it sometimes. Yesterday my boss said. 'Why weren't you in the office?' I told him to go to hell. I said I was escorting two journalists—I didn't say two English journalists. Why should I? I do what I think fit."

The pilaff comes and a young Asian we had not met before, who had grown the nails of his little fingers very long for erotic purposes, moulds pyramids of rice on his thumb and presses them into our mouths—a mark of respect. Hospitality is an abiding thing of life here. "Next time you come," Hamdam tells us, "bring wives. We don't invite bachelors to our homes because we fear for our wives. When you come again you can come to our homes. Perhaps"—he winked naughtily—"we can even swap wives."

The rain stops, the sun comes out and we drive back to Fergana and the evening plane to Tashkent. To the last Hamdam tries to persuade us to stay. His friends will be very angry with him because he has not allowed them to invite us to their homes, he says, but it's been a good holiday! He and the Director of the hotel wait to wave goodbye and they are still waving when the aircraft engines bury them in a cloud of dust.

Baku. July 22. Land smells are strong now. Yesterday we sent a telegram to Moscow booking seats on a BEA Comet to London in two weeks' time. Meanwhile we pursue our journey.

Our man in Baku is called Alexei and is possessed of a beguiling casualness which I do not altogether trust. We followed him, his straw hat thrust well back on the top of his head, on a tour of the old quarters of the city: the Maiden's Tower, the ancient Fort, last century's back-streets. "You see," Alexei said, thrusting his head through somebody's front door, "these premises are not fit to live in. We're going to pull them down and put up something more suited to modern needs." I did not agree with him, for here there was an atmosphere very remote from the gaunt blocks of new buildings of Soviet achievement. Vines crept up the walls in narrow alleys and provided shade over the streets. There were balconies covered in climbing plants and a feeling of lived-in-ness, of continuity. On one façade, written in bold letters, was an advertisement for a well-known brand of American cigarettes—residue of a location set for a Russian film company.

Late lunch and on to a new town built in the desert where only a few years ago nothing but camels lived. On the way we passed whole hillsides covered in oil-wells ticking away like grandfather clocks. The beach in front of the new town fitted my old preconceptions of the Russian scene—the blocks of flats, the cranes, the happy workers in the dirty Caspian, the jet plane screaming overhead with what looked like rockets projecting from each wing. What I had not imagined was the black sheep that stood in the sea and patiently endured a man in shorts splashing water over it; or the gigantic sunset—nature regardless of ideologies—with vermilion clouds streaming away like spokes radiating from a hub. The surrealist scene, the camera-eye incongruity of a moment of time, seems to fix itself in my mind out of all proportion to its actual significance. Why? I remember outside a Baku restaurant this morning a man in a vest clutching a hose from which water gushed at full pressure. He sat on a stool beside a tub with a pallid little tree growing in it; his eyes were fixed on this tree with an intent, unblinking and extraordinarily malevolent gaze and on to it he directed the fierce jet of water. He looked as if he was trying to kill it, like a rat in a hole. Why should I remember such a scene?

On the balcony of the hotel in the evening a Czech delegation sat at dinner. When they left, John and I took two half-empty bottles of good red wine from their table and drank them sitting on the parapet. John said: "Anywhere else"—and he looked at the lights of the bay twinkling in the water—"we would think this was a great rave. Why don't we think so here?" Why? Why this strong sense of exile? I told him I had never understood Ovid's predicament, after he was banished from Rome to the Bosphorus, till now. As we were talking a young Armenian head waiter advanced towards me with a chair. "Please sit on this," he said. "I do not wish you to fall from the parapet. You are young. It is fine to be young. The world values young people. Not that they do not appreciate old people too. But all things considered it is better to be young, and you are young. Therefore I say do not fall but sit in this chair." We both sat on chairs and he went off and brought back a little bottle of wine "with the compliments of the management". When we had all three finished it he stood up and said: "Now you must go. The restaurant closed an hour ago." I have never been so pleasantly thrown out of anywhere before.

Baku. July 23. The four of us—John, myself, Alexei and a girl journalist from Moscow called Natasha—just caught the ship to the Neftyanye Kamni oil-fields in the Caspian Sea. The sailors were hauling up the gangplank when we arrived and the Captain leaned over his bridge and bawled at us through his megaphone. The sea was still and the voyage—it took three and a half hours— was uneventful.

Neftyanye Kamni—"the Oil Stones"—is an enormous system of interconnecting piers linking oil rigs boring into the bottom of the Caspian. It now produces a quarter of all the oil produced in Azerbaijan and is two and a half times cheaper than oil brought up on land. Even here they have brought the props of Soviet living—a tiny Soviet-style square with a midget statue of Lenin and party slogans, and streets made of tubs of flowers. There is a shop, a canteen, and a cinema.

Before lunch an interview with the Deputy Director. Naturally the whole project was finished a year before schedule. Naturally the production figures were astounding. We noted the facts down. Afterwards lunch with the Director, a pleasant lunch in an extraordinary situation: in the distance oil derricks, beneath us the lapping sea breaking against the piles of the pier. Officially the oil-field is "dry", but the Director, after a certain amount of ferreting around, managed to produce a half-empty bottle of cognac.

After lunch we drove in a jeep to one of the oil rigs where they were changing a drill. Here my camera broke down and the Director of a big Moscow feature film unit, which happened to be working here, was peremptorily summoned by Alexei to come and deal with it. He came, even though it was his day off. Could it be because Alexei is a Party member? It is inconceivable that anything like it could happen with, say, a Hollywood unit. Later we went with the film Director to his quarters—five beds, a hi-fi unit, a dressing-table, and a dining-cum-work table squeezed into two small rooms. Again the astonishing contrast with the conventional Western notions of how film units should be accommodated. Could one imagine Stanley Kramer or David Lean prodding around in a casual stranger's camera? Or sitting down

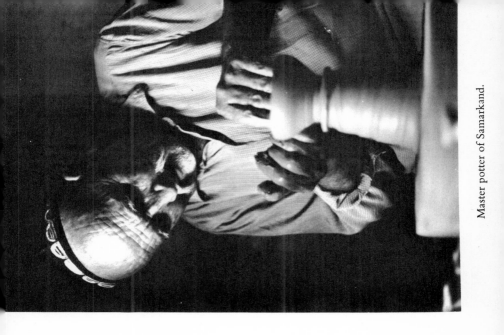

Master potter of Samarkand.

Vendor of fruit in Tashkent market.

The medieval Registan of Samarkand.

Soviet heroic and mock oriental architecture combine uneasily in this Tashkent
cinema advertising *The Three Musketeers*.

in a small room lit by a solitary bare light bulb to play dominoes, with no alcohol, no ice and not even an electric fan to keep them happy? It is very significant, very Soviet and it impressed me.

The open-air cinema was showing a new colour film that evening—a satirical fantasy about a foolish king who was plagued by an atomic mosquito—if anyone should swat it, it would explode. At the end of the film it settled on the tip of the king's nose and after a few minutes of very good comedy he died of fright in the lavatory.

The wind blew wildly in the night and shook the house where we were sleeping.

Baku. July 24. Natasha woke us at five to film the sunrise. Each one of us rose on his elbow, stared with a fixed, unseeing eye through the window and fell back heavily to sleep. Eventually we rose an hour later, filmed desultorily in a near gale and break-fasted well on steak and tomatoes and lots of tea in the canteen.

Filmed till 12.30 and caught the ship, which was supposed to have brought Simone Signoret but didn't, back to Baku. We bade goodbye to the Deputy Director, the film Director and the film Director's assistant.

Yerevan. July 25. The 7.20 a.m. flight to Yerevan takes off at 8.20 a.m. Armenia I suspect to be a *very* autonomous republic. There are few political slogans in the streets and our hotel is positively Western in style and amenities—espresso coffee bar in the foyer and a large, modern-décor restaurant with contemporary lights and mobiles and waiters who serve promptly more than one to a table. Yerevan itself is a very modern town built of soft volcanic rock called tufa. It is overlooked by Mount Ararat, which I think is as beautiful from this distance as Kilimanjaro, and in the dusk the sky is stiff with swallows, sometimes hunting in packs. View from window: the roofs and backyards of the traditional mud houses of the town, like a collection of cigar boxes, and a courtyard where I can see seven cats by three dust-bins and a dog dragging an eighth cat by its throat.

The drunk in the restaurant with the endless hiccups. "It's the Seven-Year Plan," his companions taunt. At length he rises from the table and teeters off in the wrong direction; his companions call out to him and he turns and staggers off the other way like a robot. Then there is a flurry of waiters like butterflies round a puddle and a man is hit twice in the face, falls, and limps off clutching his bloody head. All the while the band plays Italian and Latin-American popular music (*Marina Marina, I love you* and *Hernando's Hideaway*) and the guitarist crouches over the microphone and croons some old rock-and-roll numbers in English, perfect down to the adolescent sob and break in the voice. Occasionally the band plays traditional Armenian airs, but in a way that is patently derisive; perhaps they are obliged to do so, but there is no mistaking where their interests lie.

After dinner our Greek waiter beckons us into the kitchen and gives us a free drink. He came to Soviet Armenia after the war, he told us, and he'd give anything to be able to go back to Greece. But he can't. "I'm stuck in this hole like thousands of others."

Yerevan. July 26. In the afternoon to a village in the hills. Dry-stone walls, deep shade of wayside trees, cicadas chirping in the grass that grows from the earth-roofed houses, village pumps, barefoot, olive-skinned girls, old stalwarts with waxed moustaches, donkeys and ox-carts—an old, sunbaked, Mediterranean-looking world. We look at the young grapes in a wine kolkhoz and then retire to a cellar where a man siphons the best white wine from a big cask into a kettle and we (six of us) drink two kettles and eat an astringent white cheese wrapped in leaves and chupatee-like bread. The wine is delicious and we emerge into a scorching dry afternoon with heightened perceptions: colours are brighter, people are more loveable, snow-capped Ararat (rising slowly from the wide spaces of thistles and flowers, vol-canic rock and brown grass) more symbolic than ever—is this perhaps because it lies beyond the Soviet frontier in Turkey?

This morning somebody jumped from Yerevan's biggest bridge

into a deep gorge. No one would tell us anything about it—
presumably suicide is not permitted in Utopia.

Yerevan. July 27. To Etchmiadzin, the home of the Catholicos of
the Armenian Church. A large cool stone building, furnished with
Czech furniture ordered from Prague. Spoke with the archbishop
in charge of the Seminary, one of the few inhabitants of the
USSR I have met who owns a cigarette lighter. He had arrived
here in 1959 from Jerusalem after fifty-five years there. Not
surprisingly, he spoke good English but no Russian.

Then on into the interior of Armenia, through wild hills
covered in flowers—old man's beard, poppies, sunflowers the
size of a man's head. At Gegard there was a monastery hewn out
of the mountainside, where cripples begged money from Russian
tourists. From the valley below the monastery came the sound of
thumping tambourines, flutes and a woman singing songs like
the mountain songs of Greece.

We went down to join the party and found a group of peasants
sitting among the boulders by a stream in the valley bottom. In
the shade of a tree a trestle table covered in empty bottles and the
remains of a meal and seated at it a bull of a peasant, a latter-day
Cyclops, roaring and thumping the table. "He works the same
way as he speaks," his companions said, and I had visions of him,
a robot and furious blur, scything through corn like a hurricane.
We drank some beer and a young barefooted woman of coarse,
animal sensuality, her full white breasts almost tumbling out of
her green frock, sang a song for us. This is how Hemingway's
Maria would really have been; this was his band of partisan
peasants. Not lyrical love in a double sleeping-bag by starlight
but a quick grunting collision behind a bush in the heat of the
afternoon. When she finished her song there were the eternal
toasts to peace and friendship. John, weary of drunken platitudes,
chose to give a new version of them: "He says, 'Rhubarb—and
Christmas puddings. What we want is more and more Christmas
puddings.' He says, 'Ten mince pies do not make a Christmas
pudding, nor are they a substitute for rhubarb. But if we rhubarb

our mince pies we may get a pudding—and in any case our two nations—England and Armenia—should share what rhubarb we have. Only then can we have Christmas puddings throughout the world.'" I agreed and we all shook hands and drank another toast. Then trouble, a woman shouting for our Press Cards, and we beat a quick retreat up the hillside as the sound of Cyclops roaring up the valley in pursuit drew nearer. Would he have torn us limb from limb?

Doom sets in as we return to Yerevan. Film work under such conditions has become almost impossible, and in any case our cameras are falling to bits. Not so much depression as an over-powering boredom that makes one's fingers grip the edge of the table in agony—like schooldays, double Latin lessons on hot afternoons, the sound of cricket drifting through the prison windows. Let me out! Am reading *Brideshead Revisited*—the perfect antidote.

Yerevan. July 28. The young man by the fountain in Yerevan's main square. He asked us, "Where do you come from?" and we told him and fell to talking. "If I had known you were English I wouldn't have talked to you," he said. "There are so many secret police here and I expect someone will come up to me after you have gone and ask me why I was talking to those capitalists. But I love to hear English spoken." (How strange—Natasha had said exactly the same.) All the time he talked to us he was looking over his shoulder, and when three soldiers with automatic rifles walked by he lowered his head.

He was twenty-six. Two years ago he had graduated from Yerevan University but the employment officer told him he would have to work in a factory and he refused. Since then he had been out of work, supported by relatives whom he would have to repay when he found a job. "I don't have enough money to bribe the employment officer to give me a job. If I had it would be easy. You can do anything here if you have got the money. If you commit a crime and pay a bribe you don't go to prison. There are plenty of rich people—directors of shops, offices and factories—who have made their money on bribes. They could kill a man and get away with it. Oh, there are many capitalists in the Soviet Union—you should see the division between rich and poor here. For example, in Armenia the Government pays up to 100 roubles and as little as 50 roubles a month to workers. In Russia it's the same more or less. Why do they pay so little? Where does all the money go?" A high-altitude jet was streaming across the sky above us. He pointed up to it. "It goes on the armed forces, sputniks, atom bombs, political propaganda. We want to be free to earn our wages. We want to trade, to make our own livelihoods.

"There's a saying, 'Where the Armenian is, the Jew can't get on.' We have the brains of the Soviet Union—the leading astronomer, the leading nuclear physicist. We want to use them in *our* way. There are very many people here who can make first-class shoes and clothes, but they're not allowed to. Instead they have to go to work in a factory and make something else and the Government takes all the money. The result is that we have to buy Russian clothes, which are very bad. In the country poor peasants wear old-fashioned clothes—trousers with bell-bottoms, that sort of thing. They know they are old and bad but there is nothing they can do about it. We try to get foreign clothes but it's not easy. We've been buying Chinese clothes but it's difficult to get them now. Look at my shoes—they're falling to bits, absolute rubbish. When we see Western magazines and films and listen to the Western radio we begin to wonder what's gone wrong in our own country.

"Oh, our Government tells us how terrible the West is, but we know how you really live there, where I could talk to you without fear. We never wanted Communism and we don't want it now—I'd say eighty per cent of the population think the same, and ninety per cent of students. Even some of the self-professed Communists here hate Communism and the Russians—they just say they are Communists in order to get on. The real Communists are the jerks of Armenia. Maybe there are ten per cent of them. They have the power of life and death over the rest of us and they are feared and hated.

"People will tell you about the Revolution. What Revolution? In 1920 the Russian Army occupied the city and proclaimed the establishment of a Soviet Government. They did the same in Georgia, Azerbaijan and Central Asia. They didn't ask anybody, they just did it—and they call that the will of the people! So we're trapped, just like the Hungarians were—we can't do a thing. We don't have a government—just a telephone line to Moscow. Maybe we have relatives in other parts of the world but we could be sent to prison if we got in touch with them. There are many Greeks, Lebanese and other nationalities here. They all want to go back to their own countries but they aren't allowed. You think all that ended with Stalin? If that's what you think, no wonder there are so many Communists in your country.

"We detest the Russians as much as they detest the Germans and for the same reasons. Incidentally, if you go up to the left-hand side of Lenin's statue on the other side of the square you'll see that his left hand looks like his privates! Everyone knows about it, so we're not allowed to hang about the statue—the police move us on." Just then a group of Russian girls passed by. He followed them with his eyes and said, "They are the whores of the Soviet Union, the Russian girls. Give a Russian half a litre of vodka and you can knock his wife off—in his presence. In the summer *they* come pouring down here and *we* go to the Russian holiday resort at Sochi on the Black Sea. It's one way of taking revenge.

"Please, I beg you, don't repeat what I've said to anyone here. I had to say these things, they are very important. Perhaps I'm like a prisoner smuggling a message out of gaol. I don't know. These small children playing around the fountain, they are our hope for the future. If they have intelligence they will think as we do. More and more young people are going to University and there they will learn to see the truth. It's in the hands of God."

He looked almost in tears when we came to say goodbye and I felt very miserable. He was intelligent, sensitive, kindly and brave. I think perhaps he is a marked man. "Ours is a very poor country," he said as we departed. "You should go to America or France if you want to photograph something."

The question is, how many Armenians, how many Russians even, feel as this young man felt? A Westerner travelling through the Soviet Union naturally attracts dissentients and it is difficult to say whether such people are solitary extremists or persons who have plucked up sufficient courage to express openly a general, if clandestine, view. But I had no reason to disbelieve what this young Armenian had said. He spoke with profound emotion, but in a balanced way and with convictions. What he said made sense, for this country is redolent of a proud, passive resistance.

We went to the left-hand side of Lenin's statue. What we had been told about it was true. We doubled up with laughter and a policeman came up to us and said, "Do not linger on the left-hand side of the statue."

The young photographer who offered me 500 roubles for my camera. When I refused to part with it he said, "A pity. I could have re-sold it for 750 roubles." The spirit of Gulbenkian, another Armenian, still kicks strongly here. To some, indeed, he appears to be a national hero.

Tbilisi. July 29. 6.20 a.m. plane to Tbilisi, Georgia—the old Dakota-type plane, carry your own baggage. "There's a lake down there," the stewardess scolds John; "why aren't you looking at it?" "Because I'm tired," he tells her.

In the restaurant of our hotel at lunchtime there is an East German Youth Delegation. They are given plans, orders, time-tables, Intourist hand-outs, distributed like presents of candy. They all troop off to look at the wonders. I want to go home.

Tbilisi. July 30. It is now clear that the mounting chaos of our southern journey was caused by Vadim's absence from Moscow. Now things have broken down completely. There was no one in Tbilisi to meet us and no one knows we are here. John telephoned to Moscow but could get no sense out of them there. To all intents and purposes, we are lost. We have decided to cut short our expedition and return to Moscow tomorrow. In any case, we do not have the money to go to the Black Sea; it is possible we can barely raise the plane fare back to London.

Many groups of young people wandered about the streets in the warm evening. It is a delightful old town and there are more shops than you would find in an average quarter of Moscow — watchmakers, sports goods, off-licences, tobacconists, bookshops, antique shops, tailors (an overcoat of modest pretensions costs 320 roubles). One Western-contemporary building with semi-circular façade of glass and concrete actually had a bar with bar stools but steadfastly served nothing but champagne and champagne cocktails. There was a beetle on the bar counter: it wouldn't go. John jacked it up on the end of a matchstick and it walked on its front legs. Then it roared down the counter and skidded to a halt at the edge. Why am I writing about it?

We dined in an open-air restaurant under the trees, where cats foraged for scraps and two old men begged for kopecks from table to table; a man was selling melons out of a sack and across the street a youth was singing and dancing on top of a public fountain.

We walked back to the hotel in the company of two young Georgians who had just seen *This Sporting Life*. They had also seen *The Magnificent Seven* recently but preferred British to American films. They asked us what we thought of Communism and we replied that in principle we thought it was marvellous but in practice we found it very boring. They agreed. It was.

But it didn't matter. We were tired and we were going home.

.   .   .

Our journey ended there. All that was left was to return to Moscow for the last time and fly away one morning and return to the more familiar world from which we had come. We had spent four months in the Soviet Union and travelled very many thousands of miles through its immensity. It had been a long haul and we were glad, now, to go. But we had seen some of the country and met a few of the people and the blank spaces of our unknowingness were haunted with memories where once there had been only surmise. And that, at least, was something.